CHERNOBYL

CHERNOBYL

Ian Fitzgerald

This edition published in 2022 by Arcturus Publishing Limited
26/27 Bickels Yard, 151–153 Bermondsey Street,
London SE1 3HA

AD008688UK

Printed in the UK

CONTENTS

Prologue: Nuclear Accidents Before Chernobyl   7

Chapter 1: Chernobyl in Context   25

Chapter 2: The Accident   49

Chapter 3: Containment and Clean-Up   81

Chapter 4: The Investigation   117

Chapter 5: The Cost   149

Chapter 6: Collapse   175

Chapter 7: Aftermath   201

Epilogue: The Fukushima Disaster   227

Timeline   247

Index   251

Picture Credits   255

Prologue:

NUCLEAR ACCIDENTS BEFORE CHERNOBYL

If one word sums up the concerns and complaints we have about nuclear energy, it's *Chernobyl*.

It is the shadow that has hung over the atomic power industry since that terrible day in April 1986 when the facility's Unit 4 reactor, powered by U-235 uranium dioxide, exploded, releasing a poisonous, radioactive cloud that infected much of Europe, and tainted whatever good name the industry had, perhaps forever.

The story behind the Chernobyl catastrophe is one of human error, design failure, technical incompatibility, and institutional mismanagement. As such, it is tempting to think of it as a freak accident, a one-in-a-billion alignment of unique and very specific factors that could never be repeated. That's certainly the argument put forward by those involved in the nuclear energy industry, and it is plausible. But what nuclear energy's defenders don't address is that Chernobyl is just one – albeit the worst – of a series of accidents that have happened since the atomic power industry's inception in the early 1950s. And it wasn't the last power plant failure either. Accidents take place, lessons are learned, technological and safety improvements are made – and then another accident occurs. Chernobyl may be this era's byword for nuclear catastrophe, but before that, as we will see, it was Windscale and Three Mile Island. Then, in March 2011, the reactor meltdowns at Fukushima in Japan were the equal of the disaster at Chernobyl.

This does not mean, however, that the world's atomic energy nations are actively decommissioning their existing nuclear power stations or halting the construction of new ones. A few states are, such as Germany, but more countries – including France, India and China – are ramping up their nuclear energy programmes. There are also at least 30 states without nuclear power station that are planning to build them, such as Indonesia, Turkey and Egypt. For those countries committed to nuclear energy, the perceived pros of atomic power are just too tempting when measured against the cons. Once a nuclear power station is up and running it can produce electricity in a cheap and very efficient way. As a fuel source, the world reserves of uranium will outlast those of coal, oil and gas, seeing us through to the end of this century. While we wean ourselves off fossil fuels, nuclear power is the ideal transitional energy source, so the argument goes, until we develop something more sustainable and environmentally friendly. All of this, policymakers around much of the world agree, is worth the small risk of something going wrong.

But go wrong it does. In the century or so that humanity has been working with radioactivity we've had our fingers burned by it on more than one occasion – as the story of Clarence Dally will attest.

A glassblower by trade, Dally worked in the laboratory of Thomas Edison in the 1890s and assisted with the development of the great inventor's fluoroscope machine, an early X-ray imaging device that contained radioactive elements. The German physicist Wilhelm Röntgen had discovered X-rays in 1895, and almost immediately entrepreneurs as well as scientists began to search eagerly for ways to exploit the possibilities offered by the new wonder technology's ability to 'see' inside the human body. No one at the time fully understood the dangers of radiation, and scores of people like Dally willingly exposed themselves to it on a daily basis.

The first sign that something was wrong with Dally came in 1900, when his face and hands began to exhibit signs of cell damage. By 1902, severe lesions on his left hand meant he had to receive skin grafts. When these failed, the hand was amputated. Shortly after this, he lost four fingers on his right hand. 'The X-ray has affected poisonously my assistant,' Thomas Edison observed.

But these interventions did not stop the carcinoma spreading across Dally's body. First, both of his arms were amputated up to the elbow, and then to the shoulder. When he died of mediastinal cancer in 1904, Clarence Dally became America's (possibly the world's) first-ever victim of radiation poisoning, prompting the *New York Times* to declare him a 'martyr to science'. Edison regarded Dally's plight as a cautionary tale and he immediately abandoned his researches into X-rays.

But if Thomas Edison was chastened by his experiment with radioactivity, others were intrigued. In Paris, France, Henri Becquerel and the husband-and-wife team of Marie and Pierre Curie were jointly awarded the 1903 Nobel Prize in Physics for their work studying the effects of radiation. All three scientists had by this time suffered in various degree from radiation burns to the skin. Two of them – Becquerel in 1908, and Marie Curie in 1934 – almost certainly died from cancers associated with their work. (Pierre Curie died in a road accident in 1906.)

Elsewhere in the French capital, at the Pitié-Salpêtrière Hospital, an assistant named Blanche Wittmann in the institute's radiology department lost her fingers over time and then parts of her arms because of prolonged exposure to radioactivity. She died in 1913, aged 54. Ten years later, Wilhelm Röntgen himself succumbed to colorectal cancer, which may well have been caused or exacerbated by his work with radioactive materials.

Scores of other scientists and medical personnel endured burns, illnesses and in some cases death from radioactive exposure in the early years of the 20th century. But they were not alone. Keen to cash in on the public's interest in the new phenomenon of radiation, many manufacturers, from the 1910s until well into the 1930s, developed a wide range of dangerously irradiated consumer products, many of which sold very well.

These included radium-infused face creams and toothpastes, and even radioactive chocolate bars. Then there were the radium suppositories and enema treatments for people with digestive troubles, as well as the Radiendocrinator, a credit card-sized case containing around half a dozen radium-soaked pieces of blotter paper. Advertised throughout the 1920s as a means to 'invigorate sexual virility' for men, users were advised to place the Radiendocrinator inside a jockstrap or athletic support when going to bed, taking care it sat just behind the scrotum. Priced at around $12,000 in today's money, only the very rich (and the very gullible) could afford it.

The inventor of this product was William J Bailey, who was also responsible for Radithor. Created in 1918, Radithor was a water-based drink containing radium, advertised as 'Instant Sunshine'. Its makers claimed it cured impotence and various other ailments, but it fell out of favour in spectacular fashion with the death in 1932 of the American industrialist and playboy Eben Byers, one of Radithor's most high-profile champions. He drank it several times a day and is estimated to have consumed around 1,400 doses between 1927 and 1930. By the time he stopped taking it, he was already experiencing headaches and weight loss. Soon, his teeth fell out and his upper jaw and most of his lower jaw had to be surgically removed. At the time of his death, several bones and areas of tissue throughout his body had severely dissolved and holes had opened up in his skull. His demise was later reported in the *Wall Street Journal* under the pithy headline: 'The Radium Water Worked Fine Until His Jaw Came Off'.

Aside from unsuspecting consumers, another affected group were the Radium Girls of the 1920s. At Connecticut's Waterbury Clock Company, they were the workers whose job it was to draw glow-in-the-dark numbers onto the dials of clocks and pocket watches with radioactive paint. Instructed to do as neat a job as possible, they habitually licked the tips of their paintbrushes to keep the bristles tidy. As a result, it's estimated that between 30 and 40 workers died at this and similar factories in Illinois and New Jersey from mouth cancers and related diseases.

Yet despite these and other well-publicized cases and scandals linked to radiation poisoning, the general public remained largely ignorant of the dangers of radioactivity. That changed on 6 August 1945, when the United States dropped its Little Boy uranium bomb on Hiroshima, Japan, followed three days later by the detonation of the Fat Man plutonium device over Nagasaki.

Suddenly, shockingly, the world changed. The Atomic Age was born. The power and destructive energy of radioactivity had been revealed in graphic fashion for all to see.

The Japanese actress Midori Naka survived the bombing of Hiroshima but died 18 days later, and was declared the first-ever *official* victim of radiation poisoning. Within just a few days of the blast, her hair fell out and purple blotches appeared all over her body, signifying purpura, or internal bleeding. Several full blood transfusions failed to improve her condition and she passed away on 24 August from what was described as 'atomic bomb disease'. Naka was a well-known figure in Japan, and her death undoubtedly raised awareness of the dangers associated with radiation.

At the same time that physicists in the United States were using radioactive elements to develop atomic bombs, scientists there and in the United Kingdom, Germany and the Soviet

Union (USSR) were also looking at ways to harness the power of the atom to make nuclear energy.

In fact, the two programmes ran in parallel, with research in one field often proving useful in the other. Leading the way initially was the MAUD Committee. Set up in the UK in 1940, it comprised a group of scientists supervising work at the universities of Birmingham, Bristol, Cambridge, Liverpool and Oxford that explored the use of radioactive elements such as uranium and plutonium for the manufacture of weapons of mass destruction and as a potential energy source. In July 1941 MAUD outlined its findings in two papers, 'Use of Uranium for a Bomb' and 'Use of Uranium as a Source of Power', both of which laid the groundwork for future developments in both fields.

The success of Nazi Germany in the early years of World War II, followed by America's entry into the conflict in 1941, ensured that the first MAUD paper was more eagerly – and successfully – seized upon by the Allies than the second. In just four years the US-led Manhattan Project was able to build and deploy the bombs that destroyed Hiroshima and Nagasaki.

But the means by which those bombs were created also provided the machinery for developing nuclear energy, courtesy of Enrico Fermi. He was an Italian-born, naturalized American, whose role in the Manhattan Project was to find a way to unlock the huge amounts of energy contained within elements such as uranium and plutonium. He did this by building the world's first nuclear reactor, the Chicago Pile-1 at the University of Chicago.

The process at the heart of nuclear science is fission (*see* Chapter 2). This is when an atom splits, so that part of its physical mass is converted into heat energy. Fission happens all the time in nature but it's a slow and random procedure. For example, it would take millions of years for all the atoms in a lump of uranium to 'naturally' split and decay, each one disappearing in a tiny puff of heat energy. To make nuclear bombs or nuclear energy, fission has to be kickstarted and then accelerated, so that it happens when and where it's needed. In doing so it must also set off a self-sustaining chain reaction, where not just one but trillions of atoms are split simultaneously, cumulatively releasing huge amounts of heat energy – which we call radiation. Crucially for nuclear power production, that chain reaction has to be controlled to ensure that the volume of energy released can be increased or decreased as necessary, in order to avoid a deadly explosion.

On 2 December 1942 Fermi's Chicago Pile-1 reactor managed to achieve these aims: it artificially set off a chain reaction in the atoms in a piece of uranium and then controlled the spread of that reaction using neutron-absorbing cadmium control rods. The neutrons in atoms are the 'bullets' that split other atoms apart – and each time an atom splits, two or three new neutrons are created. The fewer neutrons there are flying around, the less intense the chain reaction will be. So by inserting control rods to absorb neutrons, or withdrawing them from the device, the reaction can be sped up or slowed down.

This principle of using a neutron-absorbing medium to moderate or stabilize a chain reaction is what makes nuclear power possible. But it's also what makes it dangerous. If the medium isn't suitable, doesn't work or cannot be deployed, the chain reaction will continue unabated. In a nuclear reactor, this results in a meltdown.

In this way, the history of nuclear power can be seen as the history of discovering the optimum way to moderate a chain reaction. There's much more to it, but it's undoubtedly an important issue – and it's something that's played a key role in many of the nuclear incidents leading up to the disaster at Chernobyl.

THE EXPERIMENTAL BREEDER REACTOR (EBR-I)

When the first post-war nuclear power station came online on 20 December 1951, it made a modest start, generating just enough electricity to illuminate four 200-watt lightbulbs.

To be fair, the US-built Experimental Breeder Reactor I (EBR-I) in the Idaho desert was created for research purposes, so it just needed to work rather than fulfil any practical role. Plus, a slow and steady start was thought preferable to something more ambitious, and therefore potentially dangerous. By the following day the reactor was generating enough electricity to power the facility in which it sat.

However, in November 1955, after four trouble-free years of operation, it suffered a partial meltdown. As nuclear meltdowns go, it was underwhelming, with no explosions, noxious gases or flaming reactor cores. The meltdown took place when EBR-I's operators deliberately restricted the flow of coolant into the reactor's core to see what its temperature tolerances were. They quickly discovered that the core heated up much faster than expected when not properly cooled and, as the radiation alarms sounded, the reactor was shut down and the entire facility evacuated. No one was reported hurt in the incident and little damage was done, apart from to the reactor's basketball-sized uranium core, which had partially melted.

When the reactor was rebuilt six months later, its neutron-moderating control rods (and those used in subsequent nuclear reactors) had been redesigned and made more rigid than before. The old rods were found to have been too flexible, and the movement they allowed was shown to play a part in making temperature regulation difficult inside the core.

THE KYSHTYM DISASTER

Located in the Southern Urals, close to the border with Kazakhstan, the Mayak nuclear installation had produced the radioactive fuel for the Soviets' first nuclear bomb in 1949. By the late 1950s it was well established as a nuclear 'factory', its reactors churning out weapons-grade plutonium while its reprocessing plant sifted irradiated nuclear waste for reusable fuel. It was one of the most polluted places on earth.

Under relentless pressure from the central government in Moscow to produce ever more material for atomic bombs, Mayak's managers allowed safety standards to slip to catastrophically low levels. Radioactive waste was routinely dumped in rivers, poisoning the water supply for local villages. In Mayak itself more than 17,000 workers experienced radiation overdoses during the facility's years of operation.

It is perhaps inevitable, then, that the world's third worst nuclear disaster of all time should happen in such a place, as it did on 29 September 1957. A cooling unit on a tank containing radioactive waste broke down, causing the material inside to heat up to around 350°C (662°F) before exploding. The tank's 120-tonne concrete roof was blown clean off and tonnes of radioactive material – or 20 million curies, estimated to be around half of that ejected at Chernobyl by some estimates – was released into the atmosphere across an area of 20,000km² (7,722 square miles). In the clean-up that followed, and as with

The EBR-1 reactor.

Chernobyl 30 years later, villages were demolished, 11,000 people were permanently evacuated, and thousands of animals and livestock were slaughtered. The human death toll from Kyshtym is unknown but it's thought to be several hundred, including those who later experienced radiation sickness and cancer.

Although the Soviets did a poor job managing the Mayak facility, they were much better at covering up what actually happened there, and details of the explosion did not reach the outside world until 1976. One reason why this incident is known as the Kyshytm Disaster is because it's the name of the town closest to where the accident took place. Since Mayak did not officially exist, the disaster could not even be named after it.

WINDSCALE AND 'COCKCROFT'S FOLLY'
The two British nuclear reactors at the Windscale plant in Cumbria had been built in 1950 and 1951 respectively. By 1957 they had both exceeded their planned five-year service life of making plutonium for the UK's nuclear weapons programme, so in autumn that year a plan was devised to upgrade and convert the two devices, known as Pile 1 and Pile 2, into reactors capable of producing tritium, a radioactive isotope, or element, used in powerful thermonuclear bombs.

This proved a costly mistake. One thing that was not changed in the conversion process were the graphite moderators in each reactor. One of graphite's properties is that it is able to slow the speed of neutrons, the subatomic particles that make fission possible. Once a chain reaction begins inside a nuclear reactor core, the chain reaction can be modified by introducing or withdrawing graphite into the reactor. This is most commonly done using what are known as control rods or moderators. These are long graphite-tipped poles that can be inserted into the reactor when fission needs to be slowed down and taken out when it needs to be speeded up. These graphite control rods were suitable for use with plutonium but not with tritium, and, following the conversion, they began to heat up to highly unstable temperatures.

To work around this, the plant operators adopted a process known as a Wigner release. In very simplified terms this meant heating up the reactor and then closing it down and leaving it to cool. They used this approach successfully on several occasions, but, on 7 October 1957, it failed. After shutting down the reactor in Pile 1, operators noticed that the temperature remained high. When they tried again, three days later, there was still no change.

What they did not know, but which soon became apparent, was that uranium inside the reactor was on fire and had been for at least two days. The site was evacuated and the pile's ventilators were closed, the lack of oxygen eventually putting out the fire.

Although significant amounts of radioactive iodine, caesium and xenon gases were released into the atmosphere, the Windscale episode could have been worse. When the reactors were built in the early 1950s, Sir John Cockcroft, Director of Britain's Atomic Energy Research Establishment, insisted that their chimneys be fitted with expensive and bulky filters, which he claimed would absorb radiation in the event of an accident. He was widely mocked at the time for this unnecessary extravagance, and the filters were christened Cockroft's Folly – until, that is, they were shown to have worked during the fire and no doubt helped save lives. Even so, a 1983 report by the National Radiological Protection Board estimated that

260 people may have contracted thyroid cancer because of the incident, and that 30 other victims had already died or developed hereditary genetic damage.

The government of the day played down reports of the accident to the media and stressed that it had presented no danger. The only precautionary measure taken was the withdrawal from sale of milk produced by local cows.

The Windscale incident is one reason why most nations with nuclear power programmes eventually stopped using graphite moderators in their reactors. One state that didn't was the Soviet Union, and the graphite moderators at Chernobyl would play a major role in the accident there in 1986 (*see* Chapter 2).

STATIONARY LOW-POWER REACTOR NUMBER ONE (SL-1)

To date, this is the only nuclear reactor accident on US soil that has resulted in immediate fatalities. It happened at the US Army-operated Stationary Low-Power Reactor Number One (SL-1) facility on 3 January 1961, when 22-year-old Army Specialist John Byrnes withdrew one of the reactor's control rods too far during a maintenance check. This caused a huge temperature surge in the reactor as the chain reaction inside the core accelerated.

Water inside the device vaporized instantly, causing a steam-induced pressure wave that launched the container into the air and violently ejected control rods from the device – one of which impaled Byrnes' colleague Construction Electrician Richard C Legg through the groin and shoulder and pinned his dead body to the ceiling. The boiling water and steam killed Byrnes, while another Army Specialist, Richard Leroy McKinley, died two hours later from head injuries.

As a relatively small amount of radiation was released in the accident, and, as the SL-1 reactor was sited in a remote part of the Idaho desert, no evacuation or quarantine measures were put in place following the event. In the longer term, the United States stopped making reactors based on the SL-1 design and introduced safety measures so that the dislocation of just a single control rod could not affect the reactor core's temperature.

THREE MILE ISLAND

Until Chernobyl, the best-known nuclear accident in history occurred at the Three Mile Island power station in Pennsylvania, USA, in the early hours of 28 March 1979.

In a complex and almost improbable series of events in the facility's Unit 2 reactor, pumps that fed water coolant into the reactor's core failed, causing the temperature and pressure to rise, initiating a partial meltdown. This issue should have easily been resolved by the back up pumps, but they had been switched off for routine maintenance. Compounding the issue, an automated pressure-release valve that did activate then became stuck in the 'open' position, ultimately causing pressure levels in the core to fall to dangerously low levels. This open valve also allowed water coolant, once the reactor was switched back on again, to flow in – and out – of the radioactive core, dispersing irradiated liquid not just into the reactor but into some of the facility's main buildings, too.

In addition, technicians in the control room were unable to correctly interpret the complex and ambiguous series of warning lights and signals on their display panels, partly due to their lack of training in emergency procedures. In fact, the actions they

Three Mile Island nuclear power plant.

took made the situation worse and many valuable hours were wasted as they searched for the source of the problem. By the time some semblance of control was regained, around half of Unit 2 reactor's uranium core had melted.

In time, around two million people along America's East Coast would be exposed to radiation, although no adverse health issues connected to the disaster were ever recorded. Nevertheless, following Three Mile Island, the American public's support for nuclear energy went into freefall. In 1977, just two years before the accident, nuclear power's approval rating stood at 69 per cent, its highest-ever score; in the aftermath of the meltdown it dropped to 46 per cent. For many years after the disaster, no new nuclear reactors were built, and in recent years only a handful of permits have been granted for the construction of carefully regulated facilities.

As if the accident itself was not bad enough, just 12 days before it happened, a Hollywood film was released that portrayed a potentially catastrophic near-meltdown at a fictional US nuclear power plant. Starring Michael Douglas and Jane Fonda, *The China Syndrome* dramatically showed Americans just how potentially dangerous nuclear power stations could be, at the very moment when an accident was taking place on their own soil.

As the 1970s drew to a close, nuclear energy's reputation was at a low ebb. Most people knew very little about it as a technology, and what they did know they tended not to like. But energy crises throughout the decade had shown world leaders that a reliance on other forms of fuel was a hazardous business. In 1973 the Saudi Arabian-led Organization of Arab Petroleum Exporting Countries (OPEC) stopped selling oil to nations including the United States, United Kingdom, Canada, Japan and the Netherlands in retaliation for their perceived support of Israel that year in the Yom Kippur War against an Egyptian- and Syrian-led coalition of Arab nations. With oil prices rising by up to 300 per cent, governments quickly came to see the benefit of developing nuclear-powered energy sources on their home soil.

On a practical level, this meant that nations with a diverse portfolio of energy sources would be less susceptible to pressure from their overseas fuel suppliers. In theory, it would also lead to fewer or less intense resource wars between nations. A well-resourced nuclear power sector was also essential for those nations in possession of nuclear weapons. The two industries often worked hand-in-hand, creating and supplying fuel and other resources for each other.

For these and other reasons, the Soviet Union was one of those nations that invested most heavily in its nuclear power programme. And nowhere was that investment more obviously on display than at Chernobyl. Located in western Ukraine, the plan was for it to become the largest and most powerful nuclear power plant in the world.

That never happened; what follows is the story why.

Chapter 1:

CHERNOBYL IN CONTEXT

Few people today would question Russia's status as Eastern Europe's dominant power, but it hasn't always been that way. For 400 years, from the ninth century through to the mid-1200s, power in the region resided further south.

Kievan Rus' is the name we give today to the empire controlled by the Rurik Dynasty, whose power base of Kyiv (formerly Kiev) is one of Europe's most historic cities and the capital of modern-day Ukraine. The Ruriks were Varangians, Vikings and Norsemen who had fought and conquered their way down from wintry Scandinavia and whose rule was ended only by the great Mongol invasions from Asia of the early 1200s.

When the Kievan Rus' empire finally collapsed in 1240, some of its old dependencies and imperial territories branched out on their own. One of these, the Grand Duchy of Moscow, would in time become Russia; it was ruled from 1613 by the Romanov family until the Bolshevik revolution of 1917. Kyiv and the territory surrounding it, meanwhile, endured a less stable period of rule. Over the centuries Ukraine found itself fought over and passed between the Grand Duchy of Lithuania, the Kingdom of Poland and local Cossack rulers. By the outbreak of World War I, Ukraine's former glories had long-since been forgotten, by non-Ukrainians at least.

Once the social upheavals and civil wars that followed the Russian Revolution of 1917 were over, no time was wasted in expanding their influence across the territories surrounding their country. The Union of Soviet Socialist Republics (USSR) came into being in December 1922. The fledgling republic born out of the Ukrainian War of Independence, following the collapse of the Romanov's Russian empire, was absorbed into this new 'alliance'; its government powerless against the dominance of Moscow.

Control over Ukraine was vital to the Soviet Union's survival. In strategic terms, Ukraine provided Russia with access to the Black Sea. This meant that Russia was able to station a naval fleet in the Black Sea's warm waters, from where its ships had an entry point into the Mediterranean and then the Atlantic. Without Black Sea access, Russia's naval presence in the West would have been limited to using the cold, often frozen, Baltic Sea, close to the Arctic Circle.

It's this factor that led Zbigniew Brzezinski, the Polish-American diplomat and national security advisor to US President

Jimmy Carter, to observe in the late 1970s that, 'Without Ukraine, Russia ceases to be an empire'. It's also the reason why Russian troops have been occupying the Ukrainian port city of Sevastopol and other parts of the Crimean region bordering the Black Sea since 2014.

Ever since Ukraine became independent, following the collapse of the Soviet Union in 1991, Russia has been concerned about the status of its navy. Russia's leader Boris Yeltsin signed an agreement with Ukraine in 1997 allowing his nation to use the port of Sevastopol as a base for Russia's Black Sea Fleet, but this was never enough for his successor, Vladimir Putin. In 2014, taking advantage of a period of political instability in Ukraine, Putin sent Russian troops into Sevastopol – in order, he said, to protect Russian citizens and Russian interests there. At the time of writing those troops are still in Crimea; tensions between Russia and Ukraine remain high, but for Russia the ongoing possibility of conflict with its southern neighbour is a price worth paying if it means the Black Sea Fleet can remain in place.

In addition to its geopolitical role, Ukraine is agriculturally important. About 70 per cent of its arable land is composed of earth known as *chernozem*, a mineral-rich humus that is among the most fertile soils in the world. It's why Ukraine is known as 'the bread basket of Europe'. At least, it was until it joined the Soviet Union. Beginning in 1929, a disastrous policy of land expropriation and the forced collectivization of farms across the Soviet Union – but mostly in Ukraine – saw millions of farmers and peasants displaced from the land and at least 30,000 supposedly wealthy and bourgeois landowners known as *Kulaks* executed. The badly botched consolidation of hundreds of thousands of productive smallholdings into enormous state-run farms led to a catastrophic collapse in agricultural productivity, which was followed by a famine that left at least seven million people dead, at least half of them Ukrainian.

Following World War II, Ukraine proved itself central to the Soviet Union's needs in yet another area: nuclear science. As with its military and agricultural importance, it would be another instance where the country found itself pressurized by the demands of its more powerful northern neighbour.

For reasons no one quite understands, many of the scientists involved in the late 1940s, as the Soviet Union embarked on its programmes to develop nuclear weapons and energy, were Ukrainian. Even some of those who weren't had a link to the country, most notably Igor Kurchatov, the physicist who developed the Soviet Union's first atomic bomb. Although he was Russian, Kurchatov had studied at Ukraine's Crimea State University.

It was three Ukrainian-born men in particular who played a major role in developing the Soviet Union's nuclear energy sector, and whose work and decisions would directly impact the events at Chernobyl: Efim Slavsky, Anatolii Aleksandrov and Nikolai Dollezhal.

Slavsky was an immensely powerful, yet largely unknown, figure in Soviet history. In 1957 he became director of a central government department known as the Ministry of Medium Machine Building, a position he held until 1986. Behind its deliberately dull-sounding name, the Ministry of Medium Machine Building was in fact the department responsible for the Soviet Union's entire nuclear industry. It built the state's atomic warheads, funded research programmes, built secret nuclear-weapon-fuelling plants and oversaw development of the atomic energy sector.

A level or two below Slavsky in the nuclear pecking order was the physicist Anatolii Aleksandrov, who was director of the Institute of Atomic Energy from 1960, and who would later become president of the Academy of Sciences of the Soviet Union. Slavsky and Aleksandrov were well-acquainted and shared a common goal in promoting the interests of their Ukrainian homeland. So in the early 1960s, when the Soviet leader Nikita Khrushchev (another Ukrainian) tasked the two men with accelerating the state's nuclear power programme, it was unsurprising that they turned to their fellow countryman, Nikolai Dollezhal, for help. A mechanical engineer who had been closely involved in the Soviet Union's nuclear industry from its earliest days, Dollezhal was asked by Slavsky and Aleksandrov to create a new type of nuclear reactor – bigger, better and more powerful than any yet in operation in any country. Once he'd created it, the pair thought, they would use it to build, in Ukraine, the greatest nuclear power plant the world had ever seen.

The reactor Dollezhal developed was known as the RBMK (*reaktor bolshoy moschnosti kanalnyy*, or high-power channel-type reactor). As requested, it was large and powerful, capable of generating 1,000 megawatts (MW) – enough, it was said, to power a million homes. But it was also different in crucial ways from reactors being developed elsewhere in the world in the 1960s and '70s. This was partly deliberate, as the Soviet Union could not be seen to be 'copying' the reactor designs of the decadent West. It was also partly practical, as Dollezhal was told to make his new reactor both larger and cheaper than its rivals.

The result was a device whose method of construction and operation would lead directly to the catastrophe at Chernobyl in 1986. One important difference of Dollezhal's new RBMK reactor was the decision not to surround the reactor core with a pressure vessel. This was the protective steel shell around the reactor and was intended, among other things, to absorb radiation in the event of a meltdown. It's a safeguard known in the nuclear energy industry as 'defence in depth' – which in simple terms means putting as many protective layers between a reactor core and the outside world as possible. The investigation following the Three Mile Island accident in 1979 in the United States showed that the pressure vessel at that facility significantly reduced the amount of radiation released into the atmosphere following the reactor's partial meltdown. But, in the Soviet Union, cost trumped safety. It was estimated that including a pressure vessel would double the price of each reactor, and this was an expense the authorities were not prepared to accept. Instead, a cheaper option was devised whereby the core was surrounded by a much more basic, steel-reinforced concrete sleeve that was topped and tailed with heavy steel and concrete discs. When the moment came for this arrangement to be put to the test at Chernobyl in 1986, it would not prove itself up to the task.

Dollezhal took another decision that would impact at Chernobyl: the use in the reactor core of graphite rather than water as a moderator. Following the near-disaster of the nuclear reactor at Windscale in the UK in 1957 (*see* Prologue) most nations, including the United States, had abandoned their reliance on graphite as a moderator in nuclear reactors. The Soviet Union was not among them, and Dollezhal was well aware that attempting to switch to a water-based moderator design

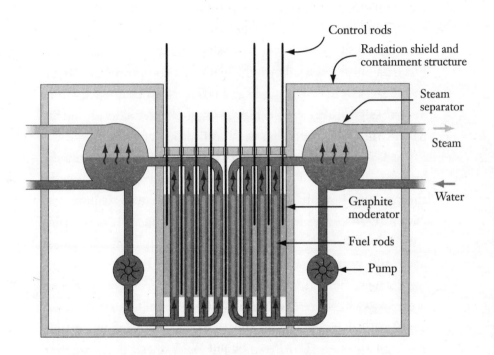

Control rods

Radiation shield and
containment structure

Steam
separator

Steam

Water

Graphite
moderator

Fuel rods

Pump

A diagram showing how the RBMK reactor works.

would have meant reinventing the entire Soviet nuclear energy strategy. Even if he had wanted to abandon the use of graphite, he would have been overruled and probably fired.

When Dollezhal delivered his new RBMK reactor in 1968, it was immediately hailed as a great Soviet invention. But this was pure propaganda. Senior Soviet officials at Slavsky's Ministry of Medium Machine Building and at the Ministry of Energy and Electrification knew about the RBMK's compromised design and the instability of graphite as a moderator but pressed ahead nevertheless. If this was reckless, so was the decision to put the RBMK into full production without thorough testing.

By 1973 an RBMK reactor was generating electricity at the Leningrad Nuclear Power Plant, near Leningrad and close to Russia's border with Finland in the northwest of the country. This directly contradicted Dollezhal's recommendation that his RBMK reactors be used only in locations as far as possible from major towns and cities, and certainly not in the western half of the Soviet Union. He did not expect his invention to fail, but he was more than aware that it could and was mindful of the fallout, actual and otherwise, if it did. He was right to be cautious. In 1975 the Leningrad Nuclear Power Plant experienced three separate reactor accidents, resulting in at least three deaths and in large amounts of radiation being released into the atmosphere. None of these incidents was reported in the Soviet media. Perhaps most worryingly, a contributory factor to each accident was a phenomenon known as the positive void effect. This was a type of failure that could only happen in an RBMK reactor and that played a major role in the catastrophe at Chernobyl in 1986.

By 1979 Dollezhal could not keep his concerns to himself any longer. In an article published in the Soviet journal *Kommunist*, he outlined his fears over possible nuclear accidents and what he saw as poor safety standards in the Soviet nuclear energy industry.

The article did not go unnoticed, and some Party officials who were not involved in the nuclear energy sector began to ask questions. Dollezhal was an immensely respected engineer and his words carried weight. He had worked with Igor Kurchatov on the Soviet Union's first atomic bomb and was intimately involved in the state's nuclear submarine programme. Moving swiftly, Anatolii Aleksandrov published a reply to Dollezhal's piece, dismissing his colleague's analysis as overstated. RBMK reactors were, Aleksandrov reassured his readers, 'as safe as samovars'. Aleksandrov knew as well as Dollezhal this was not the case, but there was nothing to be done. The Soviet nuclear power programme was too well established by then and was moving ahead with unstoppable momentum.

That had certainly been the situation in Ukraine, where as far back as 1966 senior Party men had been searching for a site on which to build the flagship nuclear power plant of Slavsky and Aleksandrov's dreams. After much searching, the place they found was definitely not one that Nikolai Dollezhal would have chosen, just 100km (62 miles) from the Ukrainian capital of Kyiv, in one of the westernmost parts of the Soviet Union. The proposed location itself was a place called Kopachi, a small village in an isolated rural spot close to the Pripyat River. It was not too far from existing railway links, which would allow building materials to be brought in by freight trains, and was close to the Pripyat River, which would provide the vast quantities of water the power plant's turbines would need to operate.

In late 1969 everything was signed off by Ukraine's leader, Volodymyr Shcherbytsky, and his deputy Oleksandr Shcherban, and funds were made available to begin the project. The first order of business, however, was to give the site a suitable name. Originally, it was going to be called the Central Ukrainian Nuclear Power Plant, but Kopachi was not in central Ukraine, so that was out. The Kopachi Nuclear Power Plant didn't work either, as the name lacked prestige. Kopachi was, after all, little more than a village, and the plant's builders wanted something that suggested history and gravitas. In that part of Ukraine there was only one place close by that had the necessary ancestry – a small but venerable town 14km (9 miles) away, known as Chernobyl.

Chernobyl first appears in the historical records in 1193, and over the centuries it had been part of Kievan Rus', the Grand Duchy of Lithuania, Poland, the Russian Empire and Ukraine. It has always been an important administrative centre and was at one time renowned as a focal point for Jewish scholarship, with a large Hasidic Jewish population. In short, it was the closest place to the reactor site with any sort of pedigree. So, the name *Chernobyl* was selected as the plant's operating title. (Ironically, after all that name searching, it was later officially decided to call the facility the V. I. Lenin Atomic Power Plant. But nobody called it that. It always was – and now always will be – Chernobyl.)

With political support secured, money made available and a large plot of land to work with, all that was needed now was a man to make it happen. Viktor Bryukhanov was a rising star in the Soviet Union's energy sector. Born in 1935 to Russian parents in Tashkent, Uzbekistan, he trained as an electrical engineer and played key roles in setting up two of that state's thermal power plants in the late 1960s. He was known to be a competent technician but was also recognized as a very effective organizer and a meticulous planner. Quiet and reserved by nature, he was well liked by colleagues who appreciated his calm and patient manner. Although just 34 years old, Bryukhanov was hired as Chernobyl's director in early 1970. This represented a major promotion for the young man, and it was his first experience working in the nuclear power area of the energy sector.

The first issue Bryukhanov encountered as he stood in the boggy fields around Kopachi was to understand the scope of his new role. He knew that he would have to manage the plant and oversee its operations – of this he had a degree of experience – but he was also expected to construct the highly complex and massive facility from scratch. This was something he had never done before and would have to learn on the job – quickly and under the ceaseless scrutiny of Communist Party bosses. Just to make his life that little bit more interesting, Bryukhanov also had to create Pripyat, an entirely new city just under 3km (1.8 miles) away, to house Chernobyl's army of workers.

Such was the importance of the Chernobyl project that Party chiefs flew in from Moscow on 20 February 1970 to clap politely as Petro Neporozhny, the Soviet Union's Minister for Energy and Electrification, wielded the first pickaxe to break ground and declare the construction site officially open. Then, once the Party *apparatchiks* were safely back in their ZIL limousines and heading back to the airport, the real hard labour began.

By all accounts the very earliest days of the project were almost idyllic, as Bryukhanov and his team put up makeshift cabins in the woods and set to work. Bryukhanov's wife Valentina joined him, as did platoons of *Komsomol* volunteers. These were members of the All-Union Leninist Young Communist League,

Viktor Bryukhanov.

all aged between 14 and 28, and their energy in clearing the ground and moving materials onto the site ensured that things got off to a good start. But it wasn't long before the professionals arrived, the builders and engineers who would actually construct both Chernobyl and Pripyat, and the initial enthusiasm of the youthful and ideologically sound *Komsomol* pioneers gave way to the more pragmatic, some would say cynical, realism of the Soviet middle-management class.

Bryukhanov took a back seat for this phase of the project, and the construction manager Vasyl Kyzyma took charge. Where Bryukhanov was introverted and self-contained, Kyzyma was outgoing and bluff; a no-nonsense foreman whose word among his men was law. Unlike Bryukhanov, he was Ukrainian, as were most of his builders and labourers, and before long a 'them and us' tension arose between the largely local construction workers and Bryukhanov's technicians and engineers, who came from all over the Soviet Union, spoke mostly Russian, and were seen by Kyzyma's rough and ready toilers as arrogant and aloof 'blow-ins' who thought of themselves as a cut about their comrades. This more or less echoed relations between Kyzyma and Bryukhanov, too, and cooperation between the two sides at all levels was grudging and rare. Kyzyma in particular rarely missed an opportunity to denigrate Chernobyl's director.

Despite Bryukhanov being nominally in charge of the entire Chernobyl and Pripyat project, Kyzyma had one important advantage over his rival: he was a much more skilled political operator. Time and again, as deadlines were pushed back or materials went missing, Kyzyma somehow managed to dodge responsibility and Bryukhanov was left to explain himself to his superiors. Theft was a particular problem at Chernobyl and thousands of tonnes of concrete, metal and machinery disappeared into the Soviet Union's black economy in the 13 years it took to complete the project.

As early as 1972, just two years into his tenure, Bryukhanov tried to quit. On top of everything else, he had just been defeated in his lobbying campaign to persuade the Ministry of Energy to use pressurized water reactors (PWRs) at Chernobyl rather than RBMKs. Although Bryukhanov pointed out that, in the event of an accident, an RBMK would produce 40 times more radiation than a PWR, the ministry responded by saying that it believed RBMKs were safer than PWRs and that they produced cheaper electricity. Bryukhanov was told in no uncertain terms that his resignation would not be accepted and that he was to see the job through to the end – and, what's more, that he would answer for any problems that came to the Soviet Central Committee's notice, now and in the future.

Bryukhanov's unhappiness was understandable. The sheer workload in managing the Chernobyl project had been wildly underestimated. Pripyat, for example, had originally been planned for a population of 12,000, rising to around 18,000 once the plant was fully up and running and all four RBMK reactors were working (by 1980, it was hoped). But those numbers were soon surpassed, and by the time the fourth of Chernobyl's reactors finally came online in 1983 Pripyat was home to 50,000 people.

In some ways the town was a victim of its own success. The 1970s and early 1980s were years of stagnation in the Soviet Union, with decades of mismanagement, corruption and a deeply flawed command economy leaving the nation on the brink of collapse. What resources the Soviet Union did have were mostly

The apartment blocks of Pripyat, the town built to house the workers of Chernobyl, have remained eerily empty since the disaster.

diverted to the military as the state desperately tried to keep pace in its Cold War arms race with the United States. As a result, for most Soviet citizens, food shortages were common, jobs scarce and wages low. But not at Pripyat. The city would enjoy special privileges as a Soviet *Atomgrad*, a place intended for the nation's brightest and best to live while they strove to make Chernobyl the greatest nuclear facility in the world. Consequently, the shops were well stocked with food and apartments were spacious. A hospital catered for the people's health needs and, in time, 15 schools and kindergartens would look after and educate the city's children. Cinemas, theatres, an amusement park, two swimming pools and even a yacht club ensured the people of Pripyat's entertainment needs were more than met.

Small wonder then that everybody wanted to live there. As more and more people arrived – mostly young, professional and scientifically minded – so the city grew, and Bryukhanov and Kyzyma, already overworked, had to build places for them to live. This was not such a problem for senior managers at the plant, including Bryukhanov, whose families were well accommodated in Pripyat's most desirable apartment building, a seven-storey edifice known locally as the White House, both for the colour of its brickwork and the VIP status of its residents. The building had its own department store, called *Raduga* (Rainbow), where luxury items, including good quality radios, French perfume, stationery, and hard-to-find car spares, were all for sale. Living even higher on the hog, Vasyl Kyzyma was one of a handful of Pripyat citizens to reside in a private house. Although Pripyat was supposedly a city where only communal, egalitarian apartment buildings were allowed, Kyzyma called in a few favours, helped himself to the necessary materials and built a handful of spacious dwellings for himself and his associates.

Yet as Pripyat began to take shape, work at Chernobyl proceeded more slowly. When he was asked why, Kyzyma bullishly explained that nuclear reactors and computerized control centres were complex and highly technical machines and that they would be ready when they were ready. But there was a lot more going on behind this perfectly reasonable statement. For a start, many of the workmen on site were not up to the job. Doors and walls were often out of alignment, finishing was poor and the general attitude prevailing was *'Close enough is good enough'*. Where the builders did take pride in their work, they too often found that they didn't have the tools or materials they needed to carry it out; these had either been stolen, had never arrived in the first place, or were faulty. On the engineering side, Bryukhanov quickly gave up asking Kyiv or Moscow to replace broken or malfunctioning machinery. Instead he set up makeshift workshops on site where his technicians foraged for parts, made running repairs and performed all manner of mechanical hacks that were definitely not part of the nuclear reactor operator's handbook.

Then, there were the impossible deadlines imposed by the Party. According to the official schedule, Chernobyl's Unit 1 reactor was supposed to be operational by early 1975; it didn't generate its first watt of electricity until December 1977. The activation of the remaining reactors was similarly tardy and it would be December 1983 before the fourth of the plant's units went online, three years later than planned. These December dates are highly significant. Under the strict regulations for building work imposed by the Party, workers and managers would be denied cash bonuses and various other perks if end-of-year targets were not met. In the topsy-turvy world of Soviet economic planning, it was perfectly acceptable for a project to be late – even extremely late – so long as it was late at the right time.

This would prove critical at Chernobyl. In the autumn of 1983, the Unit 4 reactor construction was nearing completion, but it became clear that it would not be ready and that the end of year bonus deadline would not be met unless one of the standard, but important, safety tests was postponed on the machine's turbines. Under pressure from his bosses above to get the final reactor switched on, and pushed from below by his staff to secure their end of year handouts, Bryukhanov signed the paperwork to say that the test had been successfully carried out. It had not, of course, but Bryukhanov told his engineers to make sure they didn't forget to conduct it at some point in the near future. As things turned out, it would be another two and a half years before the delayed test took place, on a day that would go down in history: 26 April 1986.

While the reactor explosion in April 1986 was undoubtedly the worst thing that ever happened at Chernobyl, it was not the first accident to have taken place there. Far from it.

In February 1979 reports reached Moscow of building irregularities and reactor problems at Chernobyl. This led to an inspection visit by Yuri Andropov, the head of the KGB and future leader of the Soviet Union from 1982 to 1984. What he found were poorly laid foundations, walls built in the wrong places and inadequate insulation against water leakage.

It is unclear what, if any, changes were made to rectify this, but, on 9 September 1982, the plant suffered its first serious accident. During a supposedly straightforward repair to Unit 1, enriched uranium was accidentally released into the reactor's core, leading to a partial meltdown. Subsequent reports on the levels of radiation released vary. An official Soviet commission concluded there had been almost no contamination at all, while an investigation by experts from Ukraine's Institute of Nuclear Research reported radiation 'hundreds of times higher' than acceptable levels. When further studies showed that the accident was probably the result of flaws in the RBMK's reactor design, the implications were too severe for Ministry of Energy and Electrification chiefs to contemplate. Instead, a reactor operator was blamed for the accident and the plant's chief engineer was fired. As official documentation blamed human error as the reason for the reactor failure, the case was closed and no steps were taken to improve the reactor design.

If anything, the Soviets accelerated and intensified their nuclear energy programme as the 1980s progressed. At the 27th Communist Party Congress in Moscow in February 1986, Anatolii Maiorets, the recently appointed Minister of Energy and Electrification, told the equally recently appointed Soviet leader Mikhail Gorbachev and an audience that included Viktor Bryukhanov of his department's intention to double the number of nuclear reactors in the USSR – and in record time. Bryukhanov and Kyzyma had already been told by Maiorets when he visited their facility at the end of 1985 that the completion date for two new reactors on the site – Units 5 and 6 – was to be brought forward by 12 months, and that in addition they were to begin planning for yet another nuclear power station across the Pripyat River from Chernobyl, which would contain six more reactors.

Whatever doubts Bryukhanov may have harboured about his new workload he kept to himself. The more volatile Kyzyma, however, was less circumspect. He told the ministry that the deadlines they imposed were unachievable, especially as the authorities repeatedly failed to deliver the building materials he needed. When this failed to produce any results, he decided to talk to the press. If this appeared to be a foolish move in a state where any form of dissent was ruthlessly crushed, Kyzyma knew that he would never have a better opportunity to voice his opinions. Mikhail Gorbachev had become General Secretary of the Communist Party of the Soviet Union in March 1985 and had begun to overturn the old order by relaxing – minimally – the Party's grip on power. Within a year in office Gorbachev was formulating his plans to liberalize the Soviet economy and allow more freedom of expression that would come to be known as *perestroika* (restructuring) and *glasnost* (openness) respectively, and Kyzyma took his chance to act.

When he was approached by the journalist Liubov Kovalevskaia, who was asking for access to Chernobyl to follow up on stories she'd heard about problems at the plant, Kyzyma agreed. Kyzyma gave Kovalevskaia permission to talk to technicians and access to data she would never ordinarily have been given. The result was an article published on 21 March 1986 in the Pripyat newspaper *Tribuna énergetika* under Kovalevskaia's pen name of L. Stanislavskaia. This revealed in detail how much of the facility's machinery, building infrastructure and hardware was defective, and explained that it was not just the plant's managers but also Soviet leaders who had contributed to Chernobyl's poor state of repair.

For Kyzyma, the article was a convenient cover for his own shortcomings because it publicly shared the responsibilities for any troubles at Chernobyl – past, present and future – among scores of politicians, officials and managers. However, it failed to generate a significant response from either the public or the authorities. The *Tribuna energetika* was a small, regional newspaper catering mostly to a readership at Pripyat, many of whom worked at Chernobyl and were already aware of the problems there.

A few days after the story appeared in *Tribuna energetika*, Kovalevskaia tried again, publishing a revised version of her article in the more widely circulated journal *Literaturna Ukraïna*. In it, her criticisms of the Soviet authorities and their complicity in the mounting troubles at Chernobyl were even more trenchant. 'The failures here will be repaid, repaid over the decades to come,' she wrote. Once more, there was a deafening silence from Moscow and Kovalevskaia's warnings went largely ignored.

What Kovalevskaia – and possibly Kyzyma – did not know was that, a month earlier, the KGB had reported to the Soviet leaders on the potentially dangerous situation at the plant, particularly regarding work on the new reactors under construction. 'As Unit 5 comes into use, the technical deficiencies discovered in the production of concrete may lead to accident-threatening situations, including the possibility of human losses,' the KGB study concluded. As with Kovalevskaia's reportage, the KGB's analysis was ignored. Presumably, Kovalevskaia and the KGB's February and March 1986 warnings were buried in the same forgotten archive as the 1981 KGB report that detailed 29 emergency shutdowns at Chernobyl since 1977, 21 of which were due to technical faults. The report unequivocally stated that the reactors' 'control equipment does not meet the requirements for reliability', but there was no follow up and no action was taken.

It seems obvious that by this time some of the Soviet Union's most highly placed officials were well aware there was something rotten at the heart of their nuclear power industry. But it was a structural malaise that could not be cured without closing down every nuclear reactor in the Soviet Union and building them again in a completely different way – rejecting the RBMK design, doing away with graphite as a reactor moderator, and introducing additional levels of protection such as pressure vessels to reactor cores. Even under Gorbachev's *perestroika*, it's unlikely this was ever going to happen in a Soviet Union that had neither the cash nor the expertise to carry it out. Too many highly placed people had too much to lose by effectively admitting that the past 35 years of energy policy had been a mistake. Until the unlikely event that something went very badly wrong, the policy was to keep fingers crossed and, if there was a problem or accident, to put the blame on human error, offer up a convenient scapegoat or two, clean up the mess – and carry on as before.

By early 1986 Viktor Bryukhanov had been the Director of Chernobyl for 16 years. The ambitious 34-year-old engineer of 1970 was now a 50-year-old veteran of the Soviet political system's relentless and ever-increasing need for *more*: more reactors, more power, more unmeetable targets, more undeliverable demands. When he returned from the 27th Communist Party Congress in Moscow in late March 1986, Bryukhanov had a whole set of new tasks to fulfil and had been reminded of the projects already in hand but which he still had to complete. This could well have been behind the decision the following month to finally carry out the long-postponed turbine test to the Unit 4 reactor. Of all the things on the Chernobyl to-do list, it was one of the easiest and most straightforward wins. What could possibly go wrong?

Chapter 2:
THE ACCIDENT

Working the night shift at Chernobyl was one of the facility's less prestigious postings. It was the time when demand for the power plant's electricity was at its lowest and the four RBMK nuclear reactors were at their least active. Technicians looking after the reactor units traditionally had little to do between midnight and 8 a.m., save keep an eye on their control panels and make sure everything was running smoothly.

The men who took care of things while their compatriots slept were used to the quiet life, and certainly preferred things that way. There were no bosses to impress, no workplace politics to negotiate, and few, if any, technical problems to worry about.

This is probably why the night-shift team members looked at each other in consternation when they turned up for work in the dying minutes of 25 April 1986. What, they thought, was

Comrade Anatoly Dyatlov doing in the Unit 4 reactor control room? Chernobyl's Deputy Chief Engineer, Dyatlov was one of the plant's most senior managers and he would normally have been tucked up in bed by now. Short-tempered by nature, Dyatlov seemed even more irascible than usual that night – and for once he had good cause.

He'd been charged with overseeing the long-delayed turbine test to the Unit 4 reactor and things were not going well. Aiming to get what was essentially a routine but bothersome job out of the way as early as possible, Dyatlov had scheduled the test for earlier that morning. He had briefed the morning-shift team and put together a plan of action. The morning crew were experienced operatives, and Dyatlov knew they would do their task quickly and reliably. With the test done, Viktor Bryukhanov and Chernobyl's other high-ranking executives could finally square it with the paperwork they had fabricated back in 1983, giving them the necessary cover they needed if any inspectors or, worse, men from the KGB came calling.

In some ways the turbine test marked a symbolic end to Chernobyl's first phase of development. It would finally allow the plant managers to regard the four original nuclear reactors as complete, ushering in a new phase; the completion of the Unit 5 and 6 reactors currently under construction would make Chernobyl the largest nuclear power facility in the world. If that was not enough, their task afterwards was to build a brand-new nuclear power station across the Pripyat River from Chernobyl, and thus seal the Soviet Union's position as the world leader in atomic energy once and for all.

With so much riding on his test, Dyatlov was a man under pressure. And that pressure only increased when the morning test was called off at the last minute. Another power station in the southern Ukrainian region of Mykolaiv had unexpectedly gone offline, so Dyatlov was told to delay his test and keep Chernobyl's Unit 4 reactor running as normal, to help make up the electricity supply shortfall. Hoping that the issue at Mykolaiv would be fixed quickly, Dyatlov postponed his test to later that same day. He contacted the day-shift leader, Yurii Trehub, told the slightly perplexed manager what he needed to do and, around 4 p.m., went home.

Trehub was not comfortable. He was now landed with a task that he had anticipated Dyatlov to have carried out, and the morning team had left some of the preparation work for the test undone. The Unit 4 reactor, for example, had been partially powered down, and Trehub didn't know whether to keep it at its current level or power it down further. The turbine test was being performed as part of a wider shutdown for the Unit 4 reactor, which was being closed that day for routine maintenance and repairs, which would see it out of action for several weeks. Trehub had arrived at work expecting to find the turbine test completed and the reactor deactivated. Neither of those things had happened and now he was being told to do them, unsupervised.

Trehub could ask Dyatlov, of course, but he knew better than to bother his volatile boss at home. Going over Dyatlov's head was out of the question, too. Asking for help was akin to admitting you were unable to do your job. In the Soviet workplace, staff were engaged in a never-ending game of Snakes and Ladders. Any sign of weakness or incompetence, below a certain level of seniority at least, was ruthlessly seized upon and exploited by rivals who wanted to take your position. So, Trehub did exactly what most Soviet middle managers in his position would have done: he sat tight and hoped the problem would go away. Fortunately for him, it did. It was not until 9 p.m. that Mykolaiv was back on stream and the conditions were right for the Unit 4 reactor test and shutdown at Chernobyl to begin. As it was now so late and he was due to end his shift in three hours, Trehub summoned up the courage to call Dyatlov at his apartment in Pripyat to let him know. To his intense relief, his superior said he would come in and oversee the turbine test and reactor shutdown himself.

One of the deputy chief-engineer's quirks was that he was known to walk everywhere, including the 3km (1.8 miles) from his apartment in Pripyat to Chernobyl, and this evening was no different. Even when he arrived at the plant, he still had some way to go. The main part of the complex was strung out along a covered walkway 800m (2,635ft) long, called the deaerator corridor. Unofficially known as the 'golden corridor' for the ribbed, bronzed metal plates that lined its entire length, it was Chernobyl's main human highway and linked the main administrative building at one end of the plant, by the entrance, with all four of the site's reactors, control rooms and turbine halls. The Unit 4 reactor sat at the other end of the golden corridor, and it was around 11 p.m. before Anatoly Dyatlov traversed its final few metres and entered the control room.

The test he was about to take on was routine but not without risk. The point of a turbine test is to assess the performance of a nuclear reactor when it experiences a sudden loss of power. Outside of a test scenario, complete power loss in a reactor would ordinarily result in an unscheduled shutdown, which was something to be avoided unless absolutely necessary. Enforced shutdowns are time-consuming, costly, embarrassing and potentially dangerous. A number of workarounds had been developed to make sure that reactors could be kept supplied with power at all times, and chief among these – in most nuclear power stations worldwide, and not just at Chernobyl – were diesel-powered backup generators.

At Chernobyl, the backup generators functioned well but typically took 45–60 seconds to become fully operational. While this is a fairly acceptable timeframe for most industries, in a nuclear power station it's 45–60 seconds too long. One consequence of a total loss of power in a nuclear reactor is that the pumps, which keep the reactor core supplied with water coolant, cease working. The reactor core is that part of the reactor containing its nuclear fuel – typically uranium – and is where the immensely powerful nuclear reactions take place. When deprived of coolant, a reactor core will quickly overheat and go into a full or partial meltdown. In short, it explodes, killing or injuring anybody nearby, and infecting a surrounding area of hundreds or thousands of square kilometres with poisonous radiation for hundreds of years.

For the physicists and technicians who ran the Soviet Union's nuclear power stations, the holy grail was to find a way to bridge the 45–60 second gap following a loss of power and keep coolant flowing into the reactor core without a break. A year or two earlier, scientific researchers in Donetsk, Ukraine, claimed they had found a solution to the backup generator problem. On paper, it certainly seemed feasible. Nuclear power stations work by inducing a chain reaction in a fuel source that will release a tremendous amount of energy as heat. This heat is used to boil water, and the steam this produces turns a series of turbines whose movement generates electricity. In the event of a total loss of power to the reactor, the steam-driven turbines would be

The Turbine Island of the Unit 4 reactor at Chernobyl, c. 1983

spinning so fast, according to the Donetsk scientists' calculations, that they would have enough residual energy to keep turning for at least one minute until they had completely run down. The plan they devised, therefore, involved switching over the function of the turbines during a power loss from generating electricity to operating the water coolant system. In this way, the reactor core could be kept cool enough for long enough to perform what is known as a SCRAM (Safety Control Rods Activation Mechanism) procedure, whereby graphite-tipped boron rods are inserted into the reactor chamber to slow down the movement of fission-causing neutrons and arrest the nuclear reaction process. This lowers the temperature in the core and avoids the need for a shutdown before the backup reactors can take over.

The trouble with the proposed solution was that it didn't quite work. In test after test, the Donetsk scientists found that

the turbines' residual energy fell just short of what was needed to keep coolant flowing for long enough to prevent a reactor from overheating. In 1985 a turbine test had been tried on Chernobyl's Unit 3 reactor and had failed again. Having reworked their calculations and suggested some technical improvements, the Donetsk scientists gave the Chernobyl engineers a new test process to follow and, by 25 April 1986, they were ready to try again, this time on the Unit 4 reactor.

One of the preliminaries necessary for the turbine test was to switch off the backup diesel generators. This was not something that would usually be done for a shutdown, but because there was a turbine test taking place as well it was deemed necessary. The nature of Chernobyl's failsafe mechanisms meant that when a power failure was detected, the backup generators automatically switched on. This was a good thing in normal circumstances, but not when attempting a turbine test. If, for any reason, there was a problem initiating the test, Dyatlov wanted the option to reattempt it straight away, which would be impossible if Chernobyl's safety systems detected an issue and activated the backup generators. Disabling important safety mechanisms was a risky strategy, to say the least, but had been approved at the plant's highest levels, going all the way up the director Viktor Bryukhanov himself.

There were no doubt a few dry throats and sweaty palms among the Unit 4 reactor control room operatives as Dyatlov finished his briefing and sent them off to their workstations. The daytime workers had gone by then, clocking off at midnight to be replaced by the less-experienced night shift. This group was led by 33-year-old Aleksandr Akimov, who had been his team's leader for only four months. Along with the rest of his shift, he was surprised at what they were now being asked to do. It all appeared to be very last-minute and rushed: their printed instructions contained crossings-out, handwritten additions and amendments by more than one person. The only consolation was that Anatoly Dyatlov was there to see them through a test that would be, in every sense of the word, major. Despite being an unpopular figure, Dyatlov was an excellent and very experienced engineer. All they had to do was follow his plan and everything would be fine.

As well as Dyatlov, there were more unexpected guests in the control room that night, including representatives from Ukraine's state energy company, visiting engineers and people from other departments keen to see how the turbine test would go. Unlike his day-shift colleagues, Yurii Trehub had stayed behind too, eager to observe the turbine test in action. In all, there were more than 20 men inside the Unit 4 reactor control room – five times the number of people usually present. This was not a problem in itself; Chernobyl's control rooms were cavernous spaces. They were dominated by the long, curving workstations that ran around each room, every surface bristling with dials, levers, winking lights, screens and buttons. An infinity of gauges and monitors covered the walls, the centrepiece was a 3m/10ft-wide circle of 211 dials called Selsyn monitors, each one showing the status and position of one of the Unit 4 reactor's graphite-tipped boron control rods. Stylistically, the room had a distinctly 1970s air, with polished crazy-paving floors and grey and beige décor, lit by buzzing, neon strip lights. A haze of cigarette smoke usually hung in the air, adding to the stale and rather dingy ambience. It was not a comfortable or welcoming environment but, at 20m (98ft) long by 10m (33ft) wide, it was certainly large enough to accommodate the increased numbers of observers present that night.

Aleksandr Akimov, as shift leader, was technically in charge, but the presence of Dyatlov in the control room blurred the lines of command – especially as the deputy chief-engineer quickly began to bark out instructions and order Akimov's men around when the reactor shutdown and turbine test got underway at 1 a.m.

The man with the crucial role of reducing power in the reactor was Leonid Toptunov. Aged just 25, he was the lead engineer on the night shift and was responsible for inserting the control rods into the reactor to slow down the nuclear fission process. Everything went as planned until Toptunov accidentally missed a key step in the operating procedure. All he did was forget to flick a single switch, but this was to have enormous consequences.

The reactor control room.

The switch operated the automatic power-reduction controller, and by not activating it – while believing he had – Toptunov ensured that neither he nor the control centre's 'autopilot' were regulating output levels inside the reactor. The result was a sudden and huge power drop, from around 520MW, about 18 per cent of the reactor's usual output, to just 30MW – a negligible 1 per cent of the reactor's full capacity.

Later on, Dyatlov claimed he had been out of the room when this happened – though he could not recall where he had been or why – and returned only when Toptunov was trying desperately to recover his mistake. Others have disputed this. In Toptunov's version of events, for example, Dyatlov was very much present throughout and began to berate him furiously when the power level began to fall. Where the two men's recollections misalign most crucially is over who made the decision at that point to

restore power by withdrawing the control rods from the reactor as quickly as possible. Dyatlov said this was all Toptunov's doing; Toptunov alleged that he was intimidated into it by Dyatlov, who reminded his younger colleague that both his job and his comfortable life in Pripyat were on the line if he failed to comply.

What is not in dispute is that it was indeed Toptunov who started the process. But the pressure of events quickly overcame him and he began to remove the control rods in a haphazard and uneven fashion. Noticing his colleague's discomfort, Trehub abandoned his role as neutral observer and rushed to Toptunov's aid. For what seemed like an eternity they struggled to restore power to the reactor, finally taking it to a low but manageable 160MW. However, in doing so they had removed 203 of the reactor's 211 rods. This was an unusual and extreme move, one that by its very nature would have a destabilizing effect on the reactor. Ordinarily, rod-removal was something to be sanctioned – if carried out at all – only by Chernobyl's chief engineer. Toptunov and Trehub were taking a huge risk in doing what they did, but in the circumstances it was their only option. Whether they were directed to do so by Dyatlov will probably never be clarified.

Although the restoration of some of the reactor's power appeared to fix the immediate problem, it had also helped to create another one. When energy levels inside a reactor fall to dangerously low levels – and 30MW was the very definition of this – the nuclear fuel inside the core becomes 'dirty' and begins to emit the gaslike isotope xenon-135. This is what happened during Toptunov's attempted power reduction. Like graphite, xenon-135 slows down the flow of neutrons, but unlike graphite, xenon-135's presence within a nuclear reactor cannot be controlled. This is one of the reasons why xenon-135 is called a 'nuclear poison': it has a purely destabilizing effect on the fission process and sends neutrons falling into what nuclear power technicians call a 'xenon well'.

The existence of xenon-135 in the reactor was reason enough on its own for the turbine test to be abandoned there and then. And yet, for reasons that are still hotly disputed, it was not. What is uncontested is that the next actions by the operators set in motion a series of events that would cause the Unit 4 reactor to explode.

After some intense discussions with a very reluctant Akimov, Dyatlov announced that the turbine test was to continue. This must have caused consternation among some of the control room operatives. To perform the test correctly, the reactor needed to be running at an output of at least 760MW. Anything less than that was a violation of official procedure. Now the reactor was barely at 200MW and was unlikely to go any higher because of the toxic effect of the xenon-135. By carrying on with the turbine test, the technicians were only creating further problems for themselves. To keep the reactor core from overheating while the turbine test was happening, reserve coolant pumps were switched on to augment the six pumps already in action. Soon, 60,000 tonnes of coolant water per hour were surging through the reactor. Water, as well as being a coolant, also absorbs neutrons, so adding more of it to a reactor already infected with xenon-135 further upset the chain reaction taking place in the core.

The reactor's power levels, previously too low, would now become too high. As temperatures rose in the reactor, the coolant water began to boil and turn to steam. In contrast to water, steam neither absorbs nor moderates (i.e. slows) neutrons. When water is converted into steam, this creates a void. A condition of more steam than water inside a reactor is known as a 'positive void'; this means there is more voided space (i.e. the volume of an area taken up by steam) than there is 'filled' space (the volume of an area taken up by water). This is when a design issue unique to the RBMK reactor came into play. In an RBMK reactor, water turning to stream allows neutrons to flow unchecked and in greater numbers. It is the RBMK reactor's fatal flaw, and it tipped the Unit 4 reactor at Chernobyl over the edge. As more and more water turned to steam, the number of neutrons increased. The chain reaction in the core grew more intense and power levels surged dramatically.

As soon as this was noticed by Toptunov, he informed Akimov. Acting quickly, the night-shift leader pushed the 'emergency only' AZ-5 button. This was supposed to initiate the SCRAM procedure that would reinsert all the control rods into the reactor. But the rapidly disintegrating state of the reactor meant that this only made things worse.

While the main body of a control rod is made of neutron-absorbing boron, the tips are made of neutron-moderating graphite. As the rods were inserted, the graphite tips displaced some of the remaining water from the reactor, so that even more neutrons now became available. In ordinary circumstances this would not have been a problem; once the main boron body of each rod was introduced, the displaced neutron-absorbing water would have been replaced by neutron-absorbing boron, so that some form of parity would have been restored. However, the skyrocketing temperatures inside the core caused the fuel assembly to fracture, distorting the rods in the process and leading them to jam in position with just the graphite tips inside the reactor.

Akimov saw that the rods were not moving and tried to override the automated insertion process, so that the rods would drop into position under their own weight, but it was too late. The rods, 7m (22ft 10in) long, remained stuck, with only 2.5m (8ft 2in) of their shafts in place. 'There was no way to explain it,' Dyatlov admitted years later. 'It was clear that this was not a normal accident, but something much more terrible. It was a catastrophe.'

At the time he told two control-room technicians named Aleksandr Kudryavtsev and Viktor Proskuryakov to head over to the reactor hall and insert the recalcitrant control rods by hand. In the investigation that followed, he claimed that he immediately regretted sending the two men out of the control room and tried to make them come back. 'I rushed after them, but they had disappeared.'

The situation was now too far gone for the graphite tips to have any moderating effect; all they did was help intensify the chain reaction in the core. The temperature inside the reactor was now around 3,000°C (5,430°F). Within seconds, output in the reactor rocketed from 200MW to 30,000MW. Both the steam pressure and the temperature were catastrophically high and, at 01:23:58 – less than 20 seconds after Akimov had tried to initiate the SCRAM safety procedure – Chernobyl's Unit 4 reactor exploded.

Back in the control room, Dyatlov and his colleagues looked at each in confusion as a low, ominous rumble filled the air and what felt like a small earthquake shook the walls. Seconds later, as they gathered their thoughts, a louder, more intense explosion blew out the lights and temporarily plunged the control room into darkness. Something very bad had happened, but what? No one at that moment suspected the reactor was gone. That possibility was unthinkable.

The control room instruments were not telling him anything that made sense, so Dyatlov waited for Aleksandr Kudryavtsev and Viktor Proskuryakov to return from the reactor hall and report what they had seen. For all its highly technical instruments, computers, consoles and gauges, one thing the control room lacked was any sort of visual link such as a video camera to the Unit 4 reactor. Had there been one, it seems unlikely that Dyatlov would have sent Kudryavtsev and Proskuryakov on what turned out to be a suicide mission.

As described in Chapter 1, the design for RBMK reactors did not include pressure vessels, which restrict the amount of radiation that leaks into the atmosphere after an accident. Instead, Soviet reactors like those at Chernobyl were surrounded by less sophisticated steel and concrete sleeves, and topped and tailed with 2,000-tonne reinforced steel and concrete slabs. This somewhat makeshift arrangement was known as a biological shield. The first of the two blasts heard in the control room was the sound of the pressurized steam finally – and literally – blowing its top, as the explosion it caused sent the Unit 4 reactor's reinforced steel and concrete lid, nicknamed 'Elena' by Chernobyl's technicians, flying straight up through the main building's roof. The airborne biological shield crash-landed back on top of the reactor, broken and skewed, leaving the core exposed and ejecting radiation into the open air.

This was bad enough but the second blast supercharged what was already a disaster and transformed it into a catastrophe. When Elena had been launched into the air, it had ripped apart the coolant pipes that were still working in the reactor, destroying any remaining possibility that the effects of the botched turbine test could be minimized. Overheating beyond imagination, the reactor exploded so violently that it blew apart the entire building. The protective graphite collar surrounding the reactor core fragmented into irradiated blocks of shrapnel that rained down 700 tonnes of material onto nearby buildings, including the turbine hall and the ventilation chimney stack shared between Units 3 and 4. All of these buildings caught fire; in some cases they would burn for at least 10 days. The core itself was on fire, as well some of the exposed nuclear fuel. Toxic smoke and 50 tonnes of vaporized nuclear-fuel particles were sent billowing into the night sky. Depending on which source you believe, they carried with them the radiation equivalent of between 40 and 300 Hiroshima atomic bombs.

Today, radiation is measured in units known as sieverts, but at that time it was calculated in röntgens. As a guide, an X-ray will expose a person to 0.8 röntgens, and the general rule for a person not undergoing any form of radiotherapy is to avoid exposure beyond 0.1 röntgens a year. Inside the destroyed Unit 4 reactor hall, the radiation level was 30,000 röntgens an hour. Being anywhere near it at the time of the explosion or immediately afterwards meant instant death.

The first victim claimed by the Unit 4 reactor was Valery Khodemchuk. A 35-year-old circulating pump operator, he had been in the pump hall next door to the reactor hall when it exploded. 'I felt a wave come through the room,' his colleague Sasha Yuvchenko recalled in an interview with the *Guardian* in 2004. 'The thick concrete walls were bent like rubber. I thought war had broken out.'

Yuvchenko had been in a nearby building when the reactor blew. He headed for the blast site to look for Khodemchuk, who had been working close to the reactor. Along the way he met Aleksandr Kudryavtsev and Viktor Proskuryakov, returning from their now-abandoned assignment to free the reactor's control rods, along with Valery Perevozchenko, an engineer and foreman at the plant. By chance, Perevozchenko had been inside the reactor hall a little earlier and had watched as the huge, 350kg (770lb) slabs covering the fuel channels feeding into the Elena biological shield had begun to rattle like lids on an overheating pressure cooker. He had been on his way to the control room to warn his colleagues that something odd was happening when the reactor blew up. The men realized they were now on a rescue mission and headed for the Unit 4 reactor hall to help Sasha Yuvchenko look for Valery Khodemchuk and any other possible survivors of what had clearly been a major accident.

'We started to look for Khodemchuk,' Yuvchenko told the *Guardian*, 'but he had been by the pumps and had been vaporized. Steam wrapped around everything; it was dark and there was a horrible hissing noise. There was no ceiling, only sky; a sky full of stars.' In another interview that same year, with *New Scientist* magazine, Yuvchenko explained what they did next: 'To get a clearer idea of what had happened we walked outside. What we saw was terrifying. Everything that could be destroyed had been. The entire water coolant system was gone. The right-hand side of the reactor hall had been completely destroyed, and on the left the pipes were just hanging.'

When they reached the flaming reactor hall, the four men in Yuvchenko's makeshift rescue party found the heavy door leading into it dangerously loose. At 1.98m (6ft 5in) and with a muscular, athletic build, Yuvchenko volunteered to brace the door open while Perevozchenko, Kudryavtsev and Proskuryakov went to look for survivors, guided inside the hall by an eerie blue-white light of radioactive particles ionizing in the night air. Seeing that the hall was completely in ruins and that no one nearby could have survived the blast, the three men withdrew almost immediately.

Those few seconds were enough to condemn them. Within a few weeks Valery Perevozchenko, Aleksandr Kudryavtsev and Viktor Proskuryakov had all died of radiation poisoning. In just a few moments they had ingested so much radioactive material that within days their internal organs began to liquify, and their deaths were slow and painful. Sheltered in the relative safety of the doorway, Yuvchenko was exposed to a lower, but still potentially lethal, dose of radioactivity – and the wounds he received were mostly to his skin. But they were terrible wounds nonetheless.

His left arm, hip and leg all suffered appalling burns where they had touched the reactor hall door to keep it open. Parts of his skin liquefied and other areas turned purple and black. In time, the tissue in his left arm died completely, and it withered to half the size of his other arm. He was subjected to multiple blood transfusion and skin grafts in the next few years and his health remained compromised ever after.

Back in the control room, it soon dawned on the operators that there had been an explosion. At first, they were unable to conceive that such a thing could happen. It was literally unthinkable: none of their education, training and working experience had taught them that reactor explosions were even a possibility. In February of that same year, Ukraine's Minister of Power and Electrification, Vitali Sklyarov, had told *Soviet Life* magazine that: 'the odds of a meltdown are one in 10,000 years. The plants have safe and reliable controls that are protected from any breakdown with three safety systems.' Unfortunately, the technicians had turned off those safety systems in order to conduct the turbine test, but such was the faith in RBMK reactors among most nuclear engineers (or those who did not know about its inherent design flaw) that the safety systems were thought to be extraneous anyway.

Struggling to process what his senses and his intuition were telling him, Dyatlov chose to believe there had been a hydrogen explosion, possibly in one of the facility's emergency water tanks. These were located directly above the control room, and he expected 11,000 litres (2,4000 gallons) of hot water to rain down on the Unit 4 reactor's nerve centre at any second. Dyatlov ordered everybody to evacuate the control room immediately and reassemble in the emergency control room nearby. But nobody moved; they were all too caught up in trying to understand the unbelievable numbers that their control panel displays were showing them.

In any case, the deluge never came. The problem lay elsewhere, as Dyatlov was about to find out in dramatic fashion when Perevozchenko arrived from the reactor hall. He was bloodied, burned, covered in poisonous dust and his skin was darkened with what would become known as a 'nuclear tan', the effect caused by exposure to excess radioactivity. When Dyatlov asked for a status report on the Unit 4 reactor, Perevozchenko told him he could not give one: it was not there anymore.

Dyatlov refused to believe Perevozchenko, and remained in denial when a turbine operator called Vyacheslav Brazhnik also came running into the control room to deliver the same news. They were both mistaken, he claimed, and what they had seen was the result of a hydrogen explosion. True, it had not occurred in the tanks located overhead, but it had happened somewhere. The reactor building may have been damaged, but there was no way the Unit 4 reactor itself could have been harmed. This he insisted, despite the fact that Perevozchenko was already visibly in the grip of radiation poisoning, continuously vomiting and passing out.

On his way back to the control room, Perevozchenko had encountered the radiation monitor Nikolai Gorbachenko, accompanied by a supervisor called Pyotr Palamarchuk. The two men told him they were searching for their colleague, Vladimir Shashenok. When they found the 35-year-old engineer, he was trapped under piles of rubble in an area known as Room 604, where the Unit 4 reactor's pressure gauges were kept. He was badly injured but still alive, and Gorbachenko and Palamarchuk suffered extensive radiation burns as they pulled the unconscious man from the debris. Ultimately, their efforts were to no avail; Shashenok succumbed to his injuries and radiation poisoning just five hours later. He was the second, and thankfully the last, person to die at Chernobyl that night.

It's a bitter irony that Shashenok should not even have been on shift that evening. This was his day off, but he had been called into work at the last minute. As he was being taken to hospital in Pripyat, a semi-conscious Shashenok kept repeating, 'I turned off the voltage… I did everything.' His wife, Lyudmila, a nurse, managed to find Shashenok before he died and was appalled by what saw. 'It was not my husband at all, it was a swollen blister,' she told an Associated Press reporter. She also remembered how Shashenok would constantly remind her that his job was not dangerous. 'In case of an accident, we have a special button,' he used to tell her.

As Dyatlov went around the control room and checked its instruments with his colleagues, everyone could see that the readings they displayed were unreliable – at best. Some control panels were inactive; others showed indicators with needles swinging wildly back and forth. Numbers were rising when they should have been falling, and falling when they should have been rising. Dyatlov paid particular attention to the reading that showed water flow in the reactor. This showed zero – not a good sign. 'Cool the reactor at emergency speed,' Dyatlov shouted, and the water pumps that had been disabled before the turbine test were restarted. The priority now was to cool the reactor (which Dyatlov still believed was working) as operators frantically tried to get as much water as they could flowing into it as quickly as possible.

This was easier said than done. After giving this instruction, Dyatlov announced he was heading to the Unit 4 reactor hall to review the situation for himself, leaving Akimov in charge of managing the water supply. But try as he might, Akimov could not get the coolant water flowing into the reactor in sufficient quantities. His stress levels must have been unimaginable. Like Dyatlov, he believed at this stage that the Unit 4 reactor was still operational and that his failure to supply it with coolant was about to send it into meltdown. The internal phone system had been disconnected by the blast and Akimov had no way of contacting colleagues around the plant to call in more help or give him a status update. Turning to Yurii Trehub, he asked the day-shift manager if he could check on the valves controlling the coolant water, to see if they had been damaged in any way.

Trehub and one of his day-shift colleagues, Sergei Gazin, went over to the hall where the valves were located but found they could not enter the room. It was filled with poisonous smoke and gas, and the radiant heat was so intense they could not get close enough to even attempt an entry.

While this was happening, Dyatlov arrived at the Unit 4 reactor hall. What he found was a hellscape of uncontrolled fires, broken fuel pipes gushing oil and irradiated water, falling debris and panicking workers picking their way through tonnes of rubble. Dyatlov was aghast. Later, in his memoirs, he wrote: 'Streams of hot water were bursting in every direction from the damaged pipes and falling on the electrical equipment. There was steam everywhere. And the crackling sounds of short circuits in the electrical system resounded as sharply as gunshots.' He was soon joined by Trehub and the two men left the building and went out into the grounds to get a clearer picture of the disaster area. 'This is Hiroshima,' Trehub told Dyatlov. 'I've never dreamed anything like this, even in a nightmare,' Dyatlov replied.

Dyatlov pondered what to do next. One of his first actions was to go into the Unit 3 reactor control room and tell staff there to initiate an immediate shutdown. He did not have the authority to do this – the order for an unscheduled shutdown could be given only by Viktor Bryukhanov – but the urgency in Dyatlov's manner convinced the operators to comply. Then, back in the Unit 4 reactor control room, he told all unnecessary staff members to leave. He knew that radiation levels in the building must have been dangerously high, but he was unable to measure them: the dosimeters that were available on site did not go high enough to give accurate readings.

Now, even though he had seen the disaster site with own eyes, Dyatlov still refused to acknowledge that the reactor was destroyed. Akimov was continuing to pump what water he could into the reactor, although there was little point, and Dyatlov did not tell him to stop. The radiation he had been exposed to was already making him feel weak and ill, and it is possible his thinking may have been impaired. Or perhaps he had simply given up. In his memoirs, which are self-serving in parts and painfully honest in others, Dyatlov admitted he knew that the reactor was dead but did not have strength to say so out loud. In any case, even if he had ordered Akimov to stop pumping water, it would have been only a temporary reprieve. Around dawn, Dyatlov's superior, Chief Engineer Nikolai Fomin, carrying out instructions issued directly from Moscow, ordered that all efforts be made to pump as much coolant as possible into the reactor.

Incredibly, almost five hours after the explosion, there were senior managers at the accident site and high-ranking politicians in both Kyiv and Moscow who were still unaware that the reactor was finished. Much of the responsibility for this lies with Dyatlov. When he admitted that he lacked the strength to say out loud that the Unit 4 reactor was dead, this was no mere rhetorical flourish. In phone conversations and in face-to-face meetings that night with Fomin and Chernobyl's director Viktor Bryukhanov, Dyatlov failed to tell them that the Unit 4 reactor had failed catastrophically and instead stuck to his story of a hydrogen explosion. This information was passed up and down the chain of command and some of the accident containment plans in response to the disaster were formulated on this faulty intelligence (*see* Chapter 3).

What this meant in the immediate short term was that two of Dyatlov's colleagues – Aleksandr Akimov and Leonid Toptunov – would be sent unnecessarily to their deaths that night. Yurii Trehub and Sergei Gazin had been unsuccessful in their earlier attempt to open the water valves into the reactor, but – with Fomin's Moscow-backed orders ringing in their ears – Akimov and Toptunov decided to try again. On reaching the feedwater room that controlled the water supply into the reactor, the two men found it semi-submerged in toxic water and leaking fuel. Wading through knee-deep irradiated liquid, they opened valve after valve until they were overcome by exhaustion and were forced to return to the control room. All this had been a waste of time: the water went nowhere; the reactor was already beyond saving. The only outcome of their labours was exposure to fatal doses of radiation. Like their colleagues Perevozchenko, Kudryavtsev and Proskuryakov, the two men would be dead within a matter of weeks.

What remained of Reactor 4 on the day after the explosion.

But if Akimov and Toptunov's heroism was ultimately futile, the efforts of other men that night were not. Dyatlov's initial preoccupation with hydrogen was correct in one respect: the plant generators were filled with highly explosive hydrogen coolant. It was clear that if the flames from the Unit 4 nuclear reactor and several other buildings reached the generators, the conflagration would be even more catastrophic. Scores of Chernobyl employees risked their lives and their health, following the Unit 4 reactor explosion, to replace the hydrogen coolant with less volatile nitrogen. They also drained thousands of litres of oil from machinery and turbines in the danger zone to prevent the fires on site from spreading further.

These efforts were led by the deputy chief of Chernobyl's electrical department, Aleksandr Lelechenko. The 47-year-old engineer took personal responsibility for turning off the hydrogen flow into the generators, returning on three separate occasions into the highly irradiated pumping station to do it in place of younger colleagues whose lives he did not want to risk. Even after being treated for radiation poisoning that night in a Pripyat hospital, Lelechenko returned to Chernobyl and resumed his damage-limitation duties once more – and then reported for work the following morning. When he died of radiation poisoning on 7 May, he became the third official fatality of the Chernobyl disaster.

By around 4 a.m. a full complement of the plant's senior executives had gathered in a secure bunker beneath Chernobyl's main administration building. This was located at the opposite end of the power plant from the Unit 4 reactor, meaning that Party officials and high-ranking Chernobyl executives could feel safe there. In all, about 40 men sat waiting for Anatoly Dyatlov to arrive and debrief them. They included Viktor Bryukhanov; Sergei Parashin, Chernobyl's head of the Communist Party committee; and, most senior of all, Volodymyr Malomuzh, the second secretary of Kyiv's regional party committee.

As soon as Dyatlov entered the room, his appearance alone was enough to tell them they were all in trouble. The deputy chief engineer was struggling with his health and gasped his way through a report that brought Bryukhanov and his associates no comfort – nor, indeed, any useful information. 'What happened?' he was asked, not unreasonably. All Dyatlov could do was shrug his shoulders in reply. He had no answer, at least not one he was prepared to give. 'I don't understand it at all,' was the best he could offer. As he stumbled through a partial and self-edited version of events, Dyatlov once more neglected to tell the disaster's key decision makers that the Unit 4 reactor was no more. He skirted the issue, handed over data readouts that most of the men assembled there may not have been able to understand, and beat a retreat.

This was the end of Anatoly Dyatlov's long night. Nikolai Fomin saw just how unwell his deputy was and had him taken away to Pripyat's hospital for medical treatment. Dyatlov's replacement was Anatoly Sitnikov, Chernobyl's deputy chief operational engineer, who had an unenviable day ahead of him. First, he had to wait and see what Bryukhanov and company in the bunker would decide. When Dyatlov staggered out of the bunker, he left behind him a confused hubbub. Out of the chaos of competing voices and opinions, a consensus eventually emerged: keep pumping water into the reactor. Dawn was approaching and still Chernobyl's experts were no closer to fully understanding or being able to effectively respond to the accident. Bryukhanov appeared uninterested, preoccupied as he was with fielding demanding telephone calls from Kyiv and Moscow. Instead of taking the lead – which was hardly in his nature anyway – he simply followed his colleagues' decision. Besides, they all knew by then that Moscow was sending down a team of experts and administrators to take charge of the disaster response and they would soon be redundant.

Sitnikov, meanwhile, had a secret. A few hours before the bunker meeting he had climbed up the equivalent of 20 storeys and looked into the collapsed roof of the Unit 4 reactor hall. He saw the reactor in flames and knew the game was up. But, like Dyatlov, he said nothing to his superiors. 'I think it's been destroyed,' he told a colleague much later that same day. 'It's blazing away. Hard to believe, but true.' Nevertheless, he continued to act is if the device was functional and, when the time came, pointlessly carried out his bunker-issued instructions to keep dousing the reactor in water.

Rather than help end the disaster, this act would serve only to make it much worse. Inside the reactor the uranium core was exposed, and highly radioactive graphite rubble lay strewn all around the reactor hall and the surrounding area. As soon as the water came into contact with any of this material, it became highly irradiated and drained down into the reactor's underground chambers and sank into the earth beneath, entering the groundwater system. Instead of helping to end the accident, this extended the catastrophic event by hours. When workers on the morning shift arrived, they were horrified to see large lumps of graphite from the reactor spread across the blast site. They could not believe that people were freely moving around the area with deadly irradiated material so close by. 'What we saw was so terrifying that we were afraid to say it aloud,' recalled Arkady Uskov, one of the engineers.

The presence of radioactive graphite from inside the reactor now laying in broken fragments outside the reactor could only mean one thing – that the reactor had definitely exploded. Even so, some still refused to believe what was self-evident. Mikhail Liutov, the morning shift's deputy chief engineer, told Uskov and others who noticed the graphite that they were mistaken, that it must have been something else. In panic, one of the operatives screamed at Liutov, desperate for him to understand. When Liutov finally conceded that it could be graphite, he argued it was probably material that had been piled up in readiness for the new Unit 5 reactor, which was under construction close by. The Unit 5 reactor graphite was checked and found to be intact, leaving Liutov to agree reluctantly that the debris he saw was indeed graphite – but still he could not bring himself to say it had come from the Unit 4 reactor. This was doublethink in action. Liutov, like Dyatlov before him, was aware of what had happened to the Unit 4 reactor – he had seen it with his own eyes – and was still able to maintain that there was nothing wrong with it. It was a useful, if not particularly healthy, psychological trick at which Soviet functionaries were especially adept. In George Orwell's *Nineteen Eighty-Four* the idea of doublethink was encapsulated in slogans such as 'War is Peace', 'Freedom is Slavery' and 'Ignorance is Strength'. At Chernobyl, Liutov and Dyatlov invented a new slogan: 'Broken is Working'.

This refusal to face facts permeated into the bunker, where Bryukhanov and the men he'd brought together to coordinate a response to the accident were doing some hard thinking. They were happy, in relative terms, with Dyatlov's assessment that the Unit 4 reactor was intact, and their priority now, before the containment and clean-up operations could fully get underway, was to prepare a statement for official Politburo consumption. Bryukhanov willingly handed this delicate task over to Sergei Parashin, and there was an unspoken understanding among everybody in the bunker that they would not interrogate too deeply the information they were being given by the men on the ground. Dyatlov's working-reactor prognosis was accepted at face value, for example, and the radiation levels were deliberately misrepresented: the dosimeters available at Chernobyl only measured on a scale up to 100 röntgens, so that was entered as the recorded rate. Bryukhanov knew the levels were much higher than that, but the readings on his dosimeters gave him the excuse he needed to allow the incorrect figure to be used.

When Parashin handed Bryukhanov the report he had prepared, with its elisions and withholdings of information, the plant director signed it, along with Vladimir Korobeinikov, the chief of Chernobyl's dosemitry department.

Shortly after this, Bryukhanov was intercepted by Serafim Vorobev, the man in charge of Chernobyl's civil defence department. Vorobev had access to a DP-5 gauge, the one dosimeter in Chernobyl with double the reading rate of the 100 röntgen devices. When he switched on the machine, it immediately went off the scale, indicating that radiation levels were at least twice as bad as those shown in Parashin's document. (In fact they were hundreds of times worse, but nobody knew that yet.) Vorobev went out into the accident site on three separate occasions to take readings with the DP-5 device and each time it completely maxed out. He even left the site and stood and watched as firefighters, plant workers, police and civilians came and went as deadly radioactive dust coated their clothing like snow. In a panic, he returned to the bunker after his final foray outside and practically yelled at Bryukhanov that the accident was much, much worse than anyone had thought.

This was news that Bryukhanov was not ready to hear. 'Go away,' he said, 'your machine is broken.' Vorobev did go, but only as far as Parashin, who also refused to hear him out. 'Go and convince the director,' he said. Deciding on one last go, Vorobev told Bryukhanov that official protocols stipulated that he declare a state of radioactive emergency and sound a warning siren throughout the plant. The last thing Bryukhanov wanted was more chaos and confusion throughout the power station, so he told Vorobev to relay his findings to the authorities in Kyiv but to say nothing to anybody at Chernobyl. When Vorobev found a telephone that worked, the civil defence official he spoke to in the Ukrainian capital refused to believe what he was saying. Having witnessed the dramatic exchange between Vorobev and Bryukhanov, Parashin approached the plant director to ask him how things stood. Bryukhanov's reply was characteristically laconic: 'Bad.'

By dawn on 26 April 1986, a clearer picture of the accident was slowly beginning to form – and already some of the men most closely involved in it were thinking of ways to minimize their role. Mistakes had undoubtedly been made, both in how the accident had been incited and in how it had been prolonged, but there would be an opportunity to investigate all of that later. The priority now was to contain the disaster and put together a plan for the clean-up.

Chapter 3:

CONTAINMENT AND CLEAN-UP

It was just a matter of minutes after the Unit 4 reactor blew that the emergency services were rushing to the accident site. One of the first people to reach for the telephone, when it was clear there had been an explosion, was Aleksandr Akimov. The blast had destroyed the control room's internal phone system, but Akimov was able to call Pripyat and ask for the fire brigade to be sent immediately. Even closer at hand were the men of the power station's own Specialized Military Fire Department No. 2 (or VPCh-2, to use its Ukrainian acronym). They were based next to Chernobyl and, at that time of night, the Third Watch was on duty under the command of 23-year-old lieutenant Volodymyr Pravyk.

They knew there had been an explosion because they had heard it – and, by the simple expedient of looking out of their station house window 500m (1,640ft) from the power station and watching as a large mushroom cloud rose up into the night sky, knew that the Unit 4 reactor was the location of the accident. The Third Watch scrambled its ZIL fire engines and was on site quickly. Pravyk was taken aback at the scale of the fire in front of him: the massive turbine hall connecting all four nuclear reactors was ablaze, and the 72m/236ft-high Unit 4 reactor building was half collapsed and in flames. Pravyk immediately radioed his headquarters with a level three alarm, the highest possible, requesting all fire crews in the Kyiv area to head for Chernobyl. By the time the first fire crews arrived from Pripyat, around 1.35 a.m., Pravyk and members of his 13-man team had already climbed onto the turbine hall roof and were tackling the conflagration from there, even as the bitumen coating the surface melted beneath their feet and threatened to tear off their boots.

None of those first responders had much understanding of the dangers of radiation. One of the firefighters, Anatoli Zakharov, remembered joking to his colleagues that, 'There must be an incredible amount of radiation here. We'll be lucky if we're all still alive in the morning.' Up on the turbine hall roof, Pravyk's colleague Leonid Shavrey kicked and threw aside lumps of debris as he fought his way forwards, unaware that what he was handling were chunks of highly radioactive graphite and uranium dioxide fuel pellets from the reactor core. As the heat intensified closer to the seat of the fire, Shavrey and his fellow firefighters removed some of their safety equipment, exposing themselves to increased levels of radioactivity. When the water from their hoses came into contact with the hot graphite and uranium dioxide pellets, the material exploded in mini blasts that released volatile hydrogen and radioactive fumes into the air.

In time, Pravyk's unit joined up with another team on the roof of the Unit 3 reactor and peered down into the open hole where the adjoining Unit 4 reactor roof used to be. After spending around 30 minutes directing hoses into the Unit 4 reactor, the firefighters were overcome with nausea and were forced to beat a retreat, vomiting and staggering barely conscious down the external metal stairway. They didn't know it, but they had all been exposed to deadly levels of radiation. The gamma and neutron radiation on the reactor roof was so intense that four minutes of exposure to it was enough to receive a lethal dose (500 röntgens per hour is deadly for humans, and emissions on the worst affected parts of the roof were 8,000 röntgens per hour).

Sometime around 2 a.m. the first medic arrived at the power plant. Twenty-eight-year-old doctor Valentin Belokon quickly established a makeshift field hospital close to the damaged reactor and began to treat the wounded so they could be sent to hospitals in Pripyat and Kyiv and, in the worst cases, airlifted to Moscow. When he was confronted by the ailing firemen, Belokon realized that it was more than fire and smoke that was making the victims at Chernobyl sick. He urgently contacted the Health Ministry and demanded he be sent potassium iodide, the drug used to treat radiation poisoning.

Back at the fire, a production line was established whereby firefighters fought the blaze for as long as their health held out, after which they were replaced by healthy new arrivals from Pripyat and from the wider Kyiv region. Eighteen fire brigades in all attended the scene over the course of the night, involving just under 200 firefighters involved and 80 fire engines. Belokon triaged the firefighters as they were stood down, deciding whose treatment could be managed on site and who needed more urgent care in hospital.

As new firefighters arrived, each wave was confronted by new issues. The melting turbine hall and reactor building roofs were one obstacle, burning hoses another: despite the water flowing through them, the heat was so intense that hoses kept bursting into flames. Then, as one localized blaze was extinguished, another one would break out: the radiant heat from the main reactor fire as well as the energy given off by the scattered fragments of irradiated graphite was causing fires to spontaneously erupt all around the accident site.

Another major problem was the water supply. The water mains feeding the hoses had been knocked out, forcing the firemen to improvise by connecting water pumps to the reservoir of reactor coolant water located some distance away. To reach the reservoir a team of firefighters had to cross an obstacle course of broken buildings, burning debris and toxic waste released by the reactor explosion. It was not until 7 a.m. that the fires around the turbine halls and the Unit 4 reactor building were under some form of control. The work put in by hundreds of firefighters, at enormous personal cost, had ensured the blaze did not spread to engulf the whole of the Chernobyl facility. If it had – if all four reactors had caught fire – the consequences are impossible to calculate.

For now, the fire was contained. The Unit 4 reactor continued to burn, and would do for another 10 days, but to all intents and purposes, the first phase of the emergency response to the explosion was over. Now the experts brought in to assess what needed to be done next had a clearer picture of the challenges ahead.

As for those first responders, many of them paid for their heroism with their health and, in several cases, their lives. Volodymyr Pravyk, the very first of the first responders to arrive in the scene, was initially evacuated for treatment in Kyiv and then, on the evening of 26 April, flown to Moscow and kept in the city's Hospital Number 6, a facility run by the state nuclear-energy agency. Shortly after being admitted to hospital, and in a rare moment of lucidity, he wrote to his wife: 'Nadya, you're reading this letter and crying. Don't. Dry your eyes. Everything turned out okay. We will live until we're a hundred. And our beloved little daughter will outgrow us three times over. I miss you both very much.' Pravyk died of radiation poisoning on 11 May. When he was buried, his body and his zinc-encased coffin were wrapped in layers of protective plastic.

As Volodymyr Pravyk and his firefighting comrades addressed the reactor explosion and its aftermath, the men who managed Chernobyl and the politicians responsible for it had to find out exactly what had happened and then put together a response.

Viktor Bryukhanov had been rudely awakened at home in Pripyat around 2 a.m. by a telephone call informing him there had been an incident of an as-yet undetermined severity at the plant. Concerned but not unduly worried, Bryukhanov took the company bus to the power station – by the time he arrived at Chernobyl and watched through the smoke and ashes as fire engines and ambulances raced to and fro, he knew that things were a lot worse than he could have imagined. His first act was to summon the rest of Chernobyl's senior executives to the plant. While waiting for his departmental managers to arrive, Bryukhanov quickly inspected the accident site. He could not – and would not – quite believe what he saw. In his first briefing inside the power plant's emergency bunker, just an hour or so after the explosion, he told his bleary-eyed team to contact each of the power plant's departments and obtain a status report.

Bryukhanov's hand surely hovered over the telephone as he made his next move, though he knew it was one that could not be avoided. As the plant director, he had the responsibility of informing Party leaders in both Kyiv and Moscow that there had been an accident. In a brief but difficult conversation, Bryukhanov was told to report back with more details as and when he had them. He was also informed that a commission of experts would be assembled to take over management of the crisis and would be sent down from Moscow as soon as possible. As soon as he put the receiver down, Bryukhanov knew that his privileged life in Pripyat, his job and his liberty would soon come to an end. Whoever else would be blamed for what happened at Chernobyl, they would share it with the power station's top man. There would be a trial and he would be declared guilty. That was the Soviet way.

But he still had work to do. After his unproductive and misleading meeting with Anatoly Dyatlov at around 5 a.m. (*see* Chapter 2), Bryukhanov was left with the definite impression that the Unit 4 reactor was still intact. He had asked no direct questions and Dyatlov had not volunteered information unprompted – both men apparently afraid to say the unsayable – and from this point onwards the actions taken by Bryukhanov and his colleagues to manage the situation were based on this false assumption. The most damaging outcome of this was the decision to prioritize the pumping of coolant water into the reactor. This was a wholly counterproductive act, which would help only to destabilize the reactor further and infect a greater area of the site with radioactivity.

The idea that the accident was not as bad as it looked had other consequences, too. One of the first Party officials to arrive in Bryukhanov's bunker was Volodymyr Malomuzh, the second secretary of Kyiv's Party Committee. Believing, like almost everybody else, that the Unit 4 reactor was not dangerously damaged, he told Bryukhanov he was overreacting when the plant director began talking about the need to evacuate Pripyat. As an old Party hack, Malomuzh knew that these kinds of decision were made elsewhere and much higher up in the chain of command. Besides, radiation levels were not spectacularly high – the (inaccurate) dosimeter readings told them so. Malomuzh repeated all of this at a meeting with Pripyat's Party Committee around 11 a.m. All they had to do, he reassured the city's leaders, was sit tight. The men from Moscow were coming and they would decide what to do next.

Those men from Moscow were led by Boris Shcherbina, the deputy chairman of the Soviet Union's Council of Ministers and the man with overall responsibity for the nation's energy sector. In the hours following the accident, a series of phone calls and hastily convened meetings between highly placed Soviet leaders resulted in the appointment of a commission that was charged with first putting together a coordinated response to the accident and then investigating its causes. At 5 a.m. on 26 April, the nation's leader Mikhail Gorbachev was woken up and briefed on the situation, which he was assured was bad but not catastrophic. Shortly thereafter, Shcherbina was told of his new role and instructed to get himself to Chernobyl and meet up with his new committee members.

Made up of nuclear experts, scientists and government officials, some of the committee men (they were all men) began arriving in Pripyat and at Chernobyl around lunchtime on 26 April – around 12 hours after the explosion. Before they arrived in Ukraine many of these committee members had been feeling quite positive. They'd been fed the official line that radiation levels at the plant were low and that the Unit 4 reactor was damaged but not destroyed. Informal chats were already taking place on the flight to Kyiv about what would happen after they had concluded their accident report: how the collapsed Unit 4 reactor hall roof could be repaired, for example, or how long before the reactor itself was patched up and generating electricity again. All of that changed when they arrived in Pripyat. Dosimeters had finally been located that were able to give accurate, or at least appreciably higher, radiation readings; the reactor was much more badly damaged than had first been thought.

The man on hand to greet the commission members at Pripyat was Bryukhanov's old enemy, Vasyl Kyzyma. As direct as ever, he wasted no time telling them what he thought of the 'marshmallow' Bryukhanov and his equally ineffective deputy, Nikolai Fomin. 'It was bound to happen sooner or later,' one commission member remembered him saying. Transported to the power plant, the commissioners were allowed to wander freely around the accident site, seeing the fire for themselves and noting the tonnes of smoking graphite that lay within the reactor's blast radius. When some of the men began to feel unwell, they made their way to the bunker to see Bryukhanov.

It was a strange meeting. While Bryukhanov and his team were happy to hand over responsibility for the clean-up to the commission, they were not willing to accept any responsibility for the accident. Everybody stuck to the story that they did not understand what had happened and the commission members present were not inclined to challenge them. This was perhaps understandable. Some of the commission members, including Shcherbina, still hadn't arrived yet, and among those already present were senior figures in the nuclear power industry: Gennady Shasharin, the deputy Minister of Energy; his boss Anatolii Maiorets; and Vladimir Marin, who advised the Soviet Union's Central Committee on nuclear affairs. All three men knew they would not be exempt from responsibility if any investigation dug into the affair too deeply, so they were prepared to tolerate a certain degree of ambiguity in the responses they received to their preliminary questions.

In addition, they all wanted this inconvenient and embarrassing episode to be resolved as quickly as possible. Maiorets gathered together the commission members who had made it to Chernobyl so far and convened a meeting with Pripyat's Communist Party committee. Although Maiorets and Shasharin intended to present a positive spin of events where they could, by downplaying the radiation levels for example, the first intimations of grim reality began to appear when Vladimir Marin asked Bryukhanov the one question the plant director did not want to answer: *If the Unit 4 reactor was still intact, where had all the graphite littering the site come from?* Bryukhanov's reply was halting and hesitant, but in the end he had to admit it could only have come from the Unit 4 reactor.

A helicopter approaches to check the damage to the reactor.

This came as close as possible to confessing that the reactor had exploded without actually saying it. And precisely because Bryukhanov did not say it, many of those present chose not to accept the obvious. 'It seemed that all those responsible for the disaster were anxious to delay as long as possible the awful moment of reckoning, when the truth would be disclosed in every detail,' was the verdict of Vladimir Shishkin, one of the Soviet officials present.

The tone of the meeting took an even darker turn when General Hennadii Berdov, Ukraine's deputy Minister of the Interior, suggested it was a good idea to prevent rail and road traffic into and out of Chernobyl. As the head of Ukraine's police force, he had in fact already put out a general notification that all police officers – and at all levels of command – were to report for duty, and before long more than 400 police personnel wearing gas masks were manning checkpoints in and around Chernobyl and Pripyat. They had also taken control of the closest train station, at Yaniv. He surprised the committee men even more when he revealed the Ukrainian prime minister, Oleksandr Liashko, had already mobilized a fleet of more than 1,000 buses in case an evacuation of Pripyat was needed.

An alarmed Maiorets tried to lower the temperature in the room, saying that talk of evacuations and cordons was premature. 'I am opposed to evacuation,' he announced. 'The danger is clearly exaggerated.' He tried to change the subject by asking to meet with Dyatlov and the other technicians from the Unit 4 reactor control room, but was told they were all desperately ill and being treated in hospital. That was not what he wanted to hear, though he seemed more reassured when he was told the reactor had been shut down. He was not a nuclear scientist and this convinced him that the danger was over.

It was at this moment that a *deus ex machina* appeared: two more commission members newly arrived from Moscow. Boris Prushinsky and Konstantin Polushkin were undoubted nuclear experts, the first the Soviet Union's chief engineer of nuclear power stations and the other a senior researcher at NIKIET, the institute where RBMK reactors had been developed. Rather than waste time on meetings, the two men had requisitioned a helicopter and flown over the Unit 4 reactor building to see the state of play for themselves. When they returned, they delivered the bad news: the reactor had blown up. As every ounce of positivity drained from the formerly bullish Maiorets, all he could ask was if there was anything that could be done. 'God knows,' said Prushinsky, abandoning 70 years of official Soviet atheism. 'There is graphite burning in the reactor. That has to be extinguished before anything else.' Just how that could be done was anyone's guess, he added.

It was early in the evening of 26 April by now and Boris Shcherbina and the final members of the investigation commission had joined the rest of their commission colleagues in Pripyat. There had been a lot of talk, discussion and argument already, but now it was time to make some decisions. Shcherbina's arrival had coincided with Prushinsky and Polushkin's revelation about the destroyed Unit 4 reactor, and the whole tenor of the meeting changed. The old official version that the reactor was damaged but working was put to rest once and for all. Under Shcherbina's chairmanship, all talk now was how to manage a nuclear device that was burning uncontrollably. After some debate it was agreed that the most workable approach was one suggested by the deputy director of the Kurchatov Institute of Atomic Energy, Valery Legasov: to douse the fire and soak up the radiation with a mix of sand, clay, lead and boron dropped onto the reactor core by helicopter. Unfortunately, it was already evening by this time and Shcherbina was told it was too dark to perform the operation safely; and in any case neither the helicopters nor the sand could be requisitioned until the following morning. As for the clay, lead and boron, they were not available at all. At least not yet. A decision was taken to begin with the sand drops as soon as possible and add in the other material as soon as they could be sourced, two or three days later. The material was to be loaded into 60kg (130lb) sandbags, and it was estimated that 50,000 of them would be needed.

As if to punctuate the urgency of this need, at around 9 p.m. that evening, while the commission members were discussing different ways of putting out the fire, the Unit 4 reactor exploded again – in three separate blasts. Until that moment the reactor had been ablaze but relatively stable, and now it was clear how volatile it could be. The cause of these explosions is still unclear, but the consensus is that it was the result of the reactor emerging, or reawakening, from what is known as an 'iodine pit'. The build-up of xenon-135 that had caused so many problems leading up to the blast had, since the explosion, provided a damping down effect on the reactivity still taking place in the nuclear core. By 9 p.m., however, this xenon-135 had dissipated and there was a corresponding increase in the reaction process – resulting in the trio of explosions that lit up the night sky around Chernobyl, sending yet more radioactive material into the atmosphere.

As the Unit 4 reactor reawakened, any idea that the people of Pripyat were safe in their homes went up in smoke. The reactor was an active volcano, and it could blow again at any moment. To make matters worse, the wind was blowing toward Pripyat from Chernobyl, and officials in the city were recording an eightfold increase in radiation levels. As Shcherbina and his colleagues waited nervously for first light, so that army helicopters could begin dumping sand onto the volatile reactor core, they argued back and forth whether Pripyat needed to be evacuated.

Shcherbina was reluctant to request an evacuation, as were several senior Soviet officials on the commission. It's likely the political ramifications of turning Pripyat into a ghost town weighed most heavily in their minds. Yevgenii Vorobev was the senior medical man on the commission and was the deputy Minister of Health. When he voted against evacuation, the argument for doing nothing appeared to be won.

The man most people on the commission credited with making the decisive case for a full evacuation of the city was Valery Legasov. As the deputy director of the Soviet Union's leading research and development centre for nuclear science, his opinion carried weight. Interestingly, he was not a nuclear scientist himself but a highly qualified inorganic chemist. This probably worked in his favour on the commission: as a scientist he could look at the evidence he was presented with rationally and objectively, but also at one remove and from an outsider's point of view. He would quickly become the public face of the commission, directing many of its actions and investigations, and presenting its reports to both the media and the politicians.

It was late in the evening of 26 April when Legasov made his first important contribution to the commission, arguing the case for evacuating Pripyat. Dramatically, he placed his hand over his heart and declared, 'I am pleading with you to evacuate the people, because I don't know what will happen to the reactor tomorrow. It is ungovernable.' Backed by Armen Abagian, a commission member who had just been to Chernobyl and had personally witnessed the three violent reactor explosions, Legasov convinced Shcherbina to call the Soviet Premier Nikolai Ryzhkov – the second most powerful man in the land after Mikhail Gorbachev – and request permission to order an evacuation.

By 1 a.m. on 27 April, almost 24 hours after the Unit 4 reactor explosion, Pripyat's civic leaders were ordered to draw up the necessary plans. The 1,200-plus buses that Ukraine's prime minister Liashko had prepared, along with 240 trucks, were soon on the road to Pripyat. The small matter of persuading hundreds of off-duty bus drivers to get out of bed and come to work was solved by the simple and very Soviet expedient of the 3 a.m. knock on the door by the security services. When told by armed police that the state required their services urgently, most drivers complied without complaint. When telling his minister of the interior Ivan Hladush to organize the transports, Liashko instructed him to act as if 'you were doing it under wartime conditions', and his deputy more than took him at his word. In hindsight it's clear that Liashko made the correct call to pre-empt the official decision to evacuate Pripyat, but at the time he faced stiff opposition – not least from his political superior, Volodymyr Shcherbytsky, the Secretary of the Communist Party of Ukraine. 'Aren't you in too much of a hurry?' Shcherbytsky asked. The implication was clear: let Shcherbina's commission decide what needs to be done and hide behind plausible deniability if anything goes wrong. Fortunately, Liashko ignored his boss and so, when the evacuation of Pripyat was finally sanctioned, it was able to proceed remarkably quickly.

In later months and years, the Soviet authorities would be criticized for the length of time it took between the reactor failure and the start of the evacuation. It's true that it could have begun in the early hours of 27 April; the buses were ready, but the politicians were not. From the moment the Unit 4 reactor exploded, the official response was marked at far too many points by long periods of denial of the scale and nature of the problem. Anatoly Dyatlov's refusal to believe his reactor had failed – could not fail – became the first narrative for the Chernobyl disaster, and those offering a different story had to campaign all the more intensely to get their point across.

So it was that just after 1.30 p.m. on 27 April, the first of Liashko's buses rolled into Pripyat, 36 hours after the reactor explosion. Some residents had already left the city by then – mostly relatives and friends of power station workers, firemen and police officers who had seen first-hand the catastrophe that had taken place and tipped off their loved ones. This was what Volodymyr Pravyk's wife Nadya and their child did shortly after the young firefighter was admitted to hospital with the radiation poisoning that would kill him – he had managed to ask his parents, who were attending him at his bedside to warn Nadya that she needed to leave the city immediately. But while Nadya departed Pripyat with at least some knowledge of what had taken place at the power station, the majority of her fellow Pripyat residents would board the buses in a state of some bemusement. The city's media had been blacked out and all workers and emergency service staff who had seen the accident site had been ordered to say nothing. Naturally, this meant that Pripyat was awash with rumours, hearsay filling the void where facts had been withheld.

Spontaneously, hundreds of Pripyat citizens began to gather outside the city's Communist Party headquarters on the morning before the evacuation. Something was in the air – and it was not just the metallic tang that more and more people could taste in the breeze drifting in from the direction of Chernobyl. At 1 p.m. Pripyat's radio station broadcast a citywide announcement for all citizens:

Attention! Attention! Dear comrades! The City Council of People's Deputies would like to inform you that, due to an accident at the Chernobyl nuclear power plant, in the city of Pripyat adverse radiation conditions are developing. In order to ensure complete safety for residents, children first and foremost, it has become necessary to carry out a temporary evacuation of the city's residents to nearby settlements of the Kyiv oblast [district]. For that purpose, buses will be provided to every residence today, April 27, beginning at 1400 hours, under the supervision of police officers and representatives of the city's executive committee. It is recommended that people take documents, absolutely necessary items, and food products to meet immediate needs. Comrades, on leaving your dwellings, please do not forget to close windows, switch off electrical and gas appliances, and turn off water taps. We ask that you remain calm, organized, and orderly during this temporary evacuation.

With just an hour's notice, the 50,000 inhabitants of Pripyat were expected to gather together one or two changes of clothes and their identity papers, and then present themselves at one of several assembly points across the city. And they did. Everybody thought they would be away for only two or three days. The proclamation was very clear about that, declaring not once but twice that this was a temporary evacuation.

Given that it had been arranged at such short notice, the evacuation of Pripyat ran like clockwork. A police officer stood by every bus, noting down the name of each passenger, and within just two hours virtually everybody was accounted for and the fully loaded buses left the city. None of their passengers would ever return. Shortly after 4.30 p.m. on 27 April, Pripyat became a ghost town.

Yet, as the buses headed away from the city, the next question was where they would go. With little time to put firm plans in place, temporary accommodation was arranged for the 44,460 citizens who were officially recorded as evacuees. Schools, social clubs and even farmsteads were requisitioned, with scores of people sleeping on floors and sharing limited washing and toilet facilities. Everybody was reassured there had not been a disaster at Chernobyl, though it looked as though there had been. Soup kitchens were set up, blankets and mattresses were delivered to the refugee sites and doctors were put on standby in case of outbreaks of communicable diseases – and to look out for evidence of radiation sickness. The lucky portion of evacuees were those who were lodged in hotels or in the spare rooms of residents in one of the 43 towns and villages where the dispossessed of Pripyat were sent.

The people of western Ukraine showed remarkable generosity and tolerance by welcoming so many of the displaced into their communities and their homes. Perhaps they would not have been so accommodating had they known of the unwanted gift the

Pripyatians brought with them; no consideration had been given to the toxic radiation that would be 'exported' by the evacuation. The clothes the evacuees wore and the few belongings they took with them were all infected, as indeed were the buses and trucks that moved them all to their new lodgings. These had been parked inside the danger zone around Chernobyl for up to 12 hours before the evacuation began, absorbing high levels of radiation. After they had completed their rescue mission, all of the vehicles were returned to their normal duties: the buses ferrying passengers around towns and cities, including Kyiv itself, and the trucks transporting goods, animals and even food across the region. It is not possible to calculate how many people were affected by this unintended consequence of the evacuation, but it cannot be assumed that there were no health issues or even deaths caused by this secondary spreading of radioactivity from Chernobyl.

Nevertheless, the evacuation was hailed as a success, proof of what the Soviet state and its citizens were capable of when called upon to act with Socialist solidarity. In reality, it was something that had been foisted on an unwilling political leadership and imposed on an unsuspecting populace. It was also unsustainable. The 'temporary evacuation' soon dragged on – from a few days, to a week, then weeks and finally months. The people had to be clothed, their children schooled, and useful employment found for everybody. Eventually, the majority of Pripyat's evacuees would be relocated to a new, purpose-built city named Slavutych, which opened 45km (28 miles) to the east of their old hometown in 1988 – and many of them would return to work at the toxic but still-functioning Chernobyl power plant in the years to come (*see* Chapter 5).

*

The logical extension of removing the people of Pripyat from harm's way was to consider the danger for the residents of other, close-by towns and villages. Airborne radiation is no respecter of city limits or town boundaries. Twenty-four hours after the clearance of Pripyat, Shcherbina's commission imposed an exclusion zone around Chernobyl and ordered that all citizens within that area leave or be removed. The commission itself had long gone by then and would find a new home in the town of Ivankiv, 50km (31 miles) south of Pripyat.

The limit of the exclusion zone was 10km (6 miles) and was imposed entirely arbitrarily. By 28 April radiation levels in Kyiv, 100km (60 miles) from Chernobyl, were already five times what they should have been, making the argument for extending the exclusion zone to the capital a strong one. But this was unthinkable. It would have involved the uprooting of tens of millions of people (to who knows where), mass panic and an immense loss of political capital among the Soviet Union's ruling class. Mikhail Gorbachev and his reformist regime had been in power for only a year; his traditionalist and hardline opponents in the Politburo and military would have seized gratefully on the sight of Kyiv's deserted streets and mothers cradling crying babies in refugee camps as evidence that their premier was not fit to rule.

There was a second point to consider: none of the Soviet Union's leaders, whether moderate or conservative, were willing to draw international attention to the accident or give an accurate impression of its scale. At least, that was the case until events early in the morning of 28 April at the Forsmark Nuclear Power Plant near Uppsala in Sweden forced their hand. When a radiation detector alarm was automatically triggered at the station, technicians there initially thought they had a leak. After some investigation it was discovered that the radiation had been carried on the wind from the southern Soviet Union. Sweden's foreign ministry asked Soviet officials for details on what this could mean and, when they received no reply, went public to ask the wider international community if other nations were reporting raised radiation levels issuing from the area around Ukraine.

That evening, the main Soviet TV news programme *Vremya* carried a brief and bland statement issued by the official Soviet media agency TASS. In its entirety, this announced that, 'An accident has taken place at the Chernobyl atomic electricity station. One of the atomic reactors has been damaged. Measures are being taken to eliminate the consequences of the accident. Assistance is being given to the victims. A government commission has been struck to investigate what happened.' It was the 21st item on the newscast and was buried towards the end of the programme, when presumably many Soviet citizens had already switched off. However, dissidents inside the Soviet Union and journalists around the globe were still paying attention. In the early hours of 29 April, Radio Free Europe and its sister channel Radio Liberty broke the story internationally, by stating that 'American journalists are reporting from Moscow that a catastrophe has taken place at the Chernobyl Nuclear power plant, not far from Kiev.' The world's media followed suit, with newspapers in the UK among the first to disseminate the story to a wider audience. 'Serious Accident Hits Nuclear Power Plant in Soviet Union,' intoned the *Financial Times* on its front page. This was as calm as the coverage got. 'Nuclear Nightmare Is Here,' said the *Daily Express*; '"2,000 Dead" In Atom Horror,' ran the *Daily Mail*; 'Red Nuke Disaster,' the *Sun* informed its readers in typically understated fashion. Within a few days the *New York Post* was claiming that 15,000 people had been killed and their bodies were being dumped in mass graves at a nuclear waste disposal site.

From this moment on, the Soviets were forced to conduct their response to the disaster with the international community looking over their shoulder. To be sure, the Soviet Union was one of the world's most closed and secretive states, but now all of Europe's most sophisticated radiation-monitoring equipment was pointed straight at Chernobyl, while the spy satellites, listening devices and the full panoply of surveillance equipment available to the USSR's enemies were focused on discovering the true nature of the accident.

By 30 April the Soviet media was still downplaying the accident. The 'settlement' of Pripyat had been temporarily evacuated, it acknowledged, and radiation levels were being carefully controlled. Events on the ground, however, had been showing this was anything but true.

The delayed military helicopters had arrived at daybreak on 27 April and immediately ran into problems. Nikolai Antoshkin, the helicopter unit's commander and a general and chief of staff of Kyiv's air force, had no troops with him apart from the pilots responsible for each aircraft. Who, he asked, was going to fill the sandbags they were going to drop into the reactor? And where was the sand? An unimpressed Shcherbina told Antoshkin to use the sand piles at the Unit 5 reactor building site. As for who would bag up that sand, that was Antoshkin's problem. Finally, after a stand-off, Shcherbina reluctantly – and somewhat vindictively – ordered two of his most senior commission members to roll up their shirt sleeves and pick up a shovel. Gennadii Shasharin, the deputy minister of energy, and Aleksandr Meshkov, the first deputy of the Ministry of Medium Machine Building, were neither of them cut out for hard labour, and by selecting them Shcherbina was stamping his authority on the group and punishing two high-ranking nuclear industry bureaucrats for allowing Chernobyl to have happened on their watch. 'He yelled at the top of his voice that we were lousy workers,' Shasharin remembered. 'He drove us like cattle... telling us that we were good at blowing up reactors but useless when it came to filling sandbags.'

Eventually, Antoshkin, Shasharin and Meshkov found more personnel to help and a sandbag-filling production line of sorts was established so that the helicopters could begin depositing material onto the fire. It was painfully slow work, though, and it was not until 29 April that an efficient system of bagging, loading and dumping was established as Young Communist Party (*Komsomol*) volunteers – the majority of them women – arrived at the power plant to give their assistance. Meanwhile, the Unit 5 reactor sand pile had been depleted and material had to be excavated from quarries nearby and delivered to each of the four airfields surrounding Chernobyl where Antoshkin's 80 helicopters were stationed.

Once the helicopters had been loaded, the difficult part of the job could begin. When they returned from flying over the Unit 4 reactor building on what they called their 'bombing runs' Antoshkin's pilots reported they were finding it difficult to see the reactor through the murk and debris of the partially collapsed structure. The tall ventilation chimney joined to the reactor building made manoeuvring difficult. The hole in the roof that they could drop the sandbags through – by hand, and one at a time – was just 5m (15ft) wide. When the airmen were able to successfully thread the eye of the needle, the plume of radioactive dust thrown up by each sandbag as it hit its target filled the helicopter cabin with toxic radiation. Little by little, improvements were made: hooks were developed that allowed sandbag-filled parachutes to be dropped onto the fire; lead plates were fitted to the helicopter floors to absorb radiation. This allowed for greater volumes of material to be dropped onto the fire more quickly, though nothing could be done to help with accuracy. It's estimated that only one in five of the pilots' loads landed inside the reactor building.

After eight long days, Antoshkin was able to inform Shcherbina that the reactor fire was, to all intents and purposes, out. His pilots had paid a high price for their endeavours, though. Most of them were experiencing radiation poisoning and several were in hospital and severely ill. Whether their sacrifices were worthwhile remains a controversial topic. At best, smothering the reactor in 6,000 tonnes of sand, lead, clay and boron did temporarily lower its temperature and prevented some radiation leaking into the atmosphere; at worst it almost led to a civilization-ending nuclear holocaust (see below). What the operation did do was have a longer-term influence on disaster response thinking. Legasov's idea of entombing the reactor in radiation-absorbing material found favour at the Soviet Union's highest levels, with Mikhail Gorbachev himself raising questions about it with his ministers. Eventually, it would develop into the longer-term and larger-scale solution for what to do with the blighted reactor when it was encased in what would come to be known as the 'sarcophagus' (see Chapter 5).

On 2 May a helicopter containing the Soviet Union's two most senior politicians after Mikhail Gorbachev flew over the still-smouldering and highly radioactive Unit 4 reactor building. Soviet Premier Nikolai Ryzhkov and Yegor Ligachev, Gorbachev's deputy on the Central Committee, had come to Chernobyl to review the work carried out by Shcherbina's commission so far. Neither man was well-versed in nuclear science and they were assailed by a barrage of facts and figures throughout their stay. Their fly-by of the burned-out reactor was the culmination of their visit, and it should have brought into focus much of the abstract information to which they had been subjected. It didn't. The presence of the two Politburo heavyweights caused some of the commission members to revert to type, and the energy minister Anatolii Maiorets, for one, could not wait to tell his superiors what he thought they wanted to hear. 'We will take all necessary measures and have Unit 4 in working order by October, and Unit 5 by December,' he informed them.

Ridiculous though this statement was, no other member of the commission dared contradict him. Instead, the meeting agenda moved on to a discussion of the radiation that was still spreading across the region. Maps were produced and it immediately became obvious that the exclusion zone around Chernobyl was too small. It is not clear who suggested extending the zone to 30km (19 miles), but this was adopted with Ryzhkov's agreement that evening. On top of the 50,000 people already removed from Pripyat, this meant another 40,000 citizens would need to be evacuated from around 80 towns, villages, hamlets and farms. The area covered was vast, encompassing more than 2,000km^2 (772 square miles). As the meeting progressed, the impossibility of repairing the Unit 4 reactor finally became clear.

It was also agreed that the ongoing 'burial' of the reactor in sand, lead, clay and boron should be upgraded, and the solution of the sarcophagus was broached for the first time.

Ryzhkov and Ligachev flew back to Moscow, leaving behind a fairly contented commission. Decisions had been made and a plan of action was coming together. Then, infuriatingly, radiation levels that had appeared to be relatively stable after General Antoshkin's helicopter operation began to rise again – and no one was able to work out why. On 5 May, nine days after the accident, radiation levels around the reactor were recorded at their highest levels yet – higher even than in the aftermath of the explosion. When the source of the radiation spike was eventually tracked down, it presented the commission with a terrifying prospect that harked back not just to the Three Mile Island disaster of 1979 but the seemingly outlandish drama of *The China Syndrome*, the film that was released at the same time.

The title of the 1979 motion picture *The China Syndrome* referred to the semi-serious belief among nuclear scientists that, in a reactor core meltdown, it was possible for the irradiated fuel to become so hot that it could burn through the bottom of the reactor, bore into the ground and, in theory, continue blazing through the earth until it emerged on the other side of the planet, in China. While few experts accepted that such a scenario was truly possible, it was conceded that a meltdown could destroy the base of a reactor building and release radioactive material into the ground, from where it could enter the water table.

If this happened, the scale of the Chernobyl disaster would increase exponentially: radiation would first poison the Pripyat River and from there not just every waterway in the Soviet Union but, quite possibly, every river, sea and ocean in the world.

Once more it was Legasov who raised this possibility with the commission. On 4 May several commission members, including Shcherbina, had been recalled to Moscow because they were beginning to exhibit signs of radiation sickness. The man overseeing the commission's work in Chernobyl was now Ivan Silayev, a senior Politburo member who, in 1991, would briefly become prime minister of the Soviet Union. Advised by Legasov, Silayev informed Shcherbina, now recuperating in Moscow, that they had found the probable cause of the rising radiation levels, and that it was a problem of their own making. By continuing to pump tens of thousands of gallons of coolant into the destroyed reactor for hours after it exploded, under direct instruction from Moscow, the men who had tried to contain the damage had unwittingly created a vast lake of highly irradiated water underneath the burning building. That water was now heating up and, if it began to boil and turn to steam, there was a very real danger it could induce another catastrophic explosion in the highly unstable reactor.

When Valery Legasov sat down and considered what this meant, he came to some worrying conclusions. He calculated that the Unit 4 reactor had originally contained 2,500 tonnes of graphite, some of which had been violently ejected in the initial explosion and strewn haphazardly around the blast zone. What was left inside the reactor, he estimated, was on fire and burning at a temperature of around 1,000 °C (1,832 °F). The heat and intense radiation would soon melt the protective casing, or 'casettes', around the containers, which held the reactor's uranium dioxide fuel. Once these were exposed, radioactive particles, known as radionuclides, would be released unchecked into the air. If the remaining graphite left in the reactor continued to burn at its current rate of around one tonne an hour, the fire would continue to burn for at least eight weeks and produce enough contaminant to spread across the world for several years. That was a conservative reckoning. Alternatively, if the boiling lake of water under the reactor did reach a critical stage, producing steam that led to another positive-void nuclear reaction, this whole process would be massively accelerated. Instead of a slow release of radioactivity over eight weeks, there would instead be an explosion releasing it all in a single instant – taking out the other three nuclear reactors at Chernobyl at the same time. In short, a massive nuclear cataclysm, with world-changing consequences.

To add insult to injury, it was Legasov's original plan of dumping sand and other material into the reactor that was making this nightmare event more likely. Although the bombing runs performed by General Antoshkin's helicopter crews initially seemed to placate the angry reactor, it was now thought that the nearly 6,000 tonnes of sand, clay, lead and boron weighing heavily on top of the nuclear core were beginning to fuse in the intense heat into a destabilizing ooze that could actually provoke an uncontrollable chain reaction. Compressed from above by a volatile sludge and cooked from below by irradiated water, the reactor was now even more dangerous than at the time of the explosion. If it went again, it could erupt both outward and downward — a scenario that did not bear thinking about: Hiroshima meets *The China Syndrome*.

Legasov took his findings to Silayev and told him the only way to prevent any of this happening was to drain the water coolant lake that had formed under the reactor. Not surprisingly, Silayev dropped everything to put this potentially planet-saving plan into action. A squadron of men, led by an heroic officer named Captain Piotr 'Moose' Zborovsky, was sent in to dig through the rubble under the Unit 4 reactor, wade into the toxic water now 4m (13ft) deep and pump out thousands of cubic metres of irradiated liquid. This was a perilous commission and most of the men involved suffered ill health and premature death in the years that followed. 'Moose' Zborovsky, a man famed for his physical prowess, died in 2007 aged 55, his bones by then brittle and weak. When the men had finished their work, three specialist engineers were ordered into the area under the reactor to check radiation levels and to open a series of drainage valves to ensure the chamber could not fill with water again. Miraculously, the three engineers – Boris Baranov, Alexey Ananenko and Valery Bespalov – suffered no ill effects from their descent into Chernobyl's underworld.

With the underside of the Unit 4 reactor safely drained, the next step was to somehow fortify the area beneath the reactor to ensure a *China Syndrome* scenario could not occur. After several ideas were proposed and rejected, it was agreed that a concrete-roofed vault, with an area of 30m^2 (320ft^2), should be dug under the reactor and a fitted with a custom-made heat exchanger. Essentially an oversized air-conditioning unit, the heat exchanger was designed to keep the base of the reactor cool and prevent temperatures inside from becoming dangerously high.

Digging out the chamber would be hot, dangerous and back-breaking work. Almost 400 miners were shipped in from Ukraine's Donbas area and Tula, a region a couple of hundred kilometres south of Moscow, and set to work. First, they began to sink a tunnel, starting 130m (425ft) from the reactor. This allowed them to dig deep enough so that they would be protected from the worst effects of the radiation as they approached their destination. Their workspace was just 180cm (71in) in diameter and it was as hot as an oven. Most of the miners worked naked. They set up homemade underground railway trolleys to remove the soil and rocks they hacked out by hand – some 40–50 tonnes in each three-hour shift.

   It took several weeks to complete the tunnel and the heat-exchanger chamber, and the device itself was welded together piece by piece inside the vault by specialist engineers. This added to the heat and fumes inside the confined space, and the engineers were able to work for only a few minutes at a time before they began to pass out. It was difficult and laborious work and it was not until 24 June, more than two months after the explosion, that the heat exchanger was ready to be switched on. It never was. By this time temperatures and radiation rates inside the broken reactor had fallen to what were considered acceptable levels and the device was written off as surplus to requirements. The hard work, and the danger, to which the miners and engineers had exposed themselves, had all been for nothing.

It was around this time that a new name was coined for the operatives brought in to fix the many problems caused by the reactor explosion: liquidators. Some of these people were liquidators in the literal sense, such as the squads of men who were sent into Pripyat and the surrounding countryside to shoot dead the many dogs, cats and other abandoned pets and livestock that had been left behind by the evacuated populace. It was grim work, but it was deemed necessary by the authorities who believed that infected animals if left alive would spread radioactivity – through particles contained in their fur, through their bodily excretions and through breeding. The other type of liquidators found at Chernobyl were those brought in to perform specific clean-up roles that, one by one, would 'liquidate' the problems thrown up by the reactor failure: General Antoshkin's helicopter pilots, for example, or the Donbas and Tula miners.

As time wore on, more and more liquidators were brought into the exclusion zone to help with the clean-up. It was a dual process of decontamination and destruction. Helicopter pilots doused infected buildings within the exclusion zone with a substance known as 'water soup', designed to made radioactive particles stick to surfaces rather than fly or float freely into the atmosphere. Troops on the ground sprayed entire abandoned towns and villages with decontaminant and ploughed contaminated crops into the ground to prevent their seeds from germinating and disseminating. Whole forests were bulldozed and, where villages were thought to be too infected to be saved, they were razed to the ground. Most notoriously – and dangerously – young army liquidators were sent up onto the roofs of the Unit 3 reactor and what was left of the Unit 4 reactor to clear them of contaminated graphite and gamma ray-emitting uranium dioxide fuel that had been dumped there by the explosion. So long as hot and irradiated graphite littered the Unit 3 and Unit 4 roofs, the former's reactor could not be restarted and the sarcophagus for the latter could not be completed (*see* Chapter 7).

A small army of 3,000 men, under the control of General Nikolai Tarakanov, worked in shifts for days to physically move each piece of rubble. Initially, radio-controlled robotic devices were used to clear the roofs, but they kept breaking down or

A liquidator at work during decontamination activities.

struggled to navigate the debris under their wheels. It was quickly decided that only humans would be able to do this dangerous work properly where the radio-controlled devices couldn't. In a grim instance of gallows humour, the young men replacing the mechanical robots were dubbed 'biorobots', and the name stuck. Each biorobot, clad in an improvised 'armour' of gas masks and lead aprons, was handed a shovel and told to run out onto the roof and dump as much graphite over the side of the building as they could in no more than 30 seconds. When their time was up, each soldier had to run back to the relative safety of the building's stairwell and get himself sprayed with decontaminant, then prepare himself to go again. This was a brave and, most experts now agree, unnecessary operation. Radiation levels remained too high for another 12 months for the Unit 3 reactor to be used, even when the roof had been cleared, and in the process hundreds of soldiers had their health irreparably damaged. It did mean that the sarcophagus for the ruined Unit 4 reactor could be finished, though.

Even so, the clearance operation carried out by General Tarakanov's team of biorobots was celebrated at the time as part of the wider success of the containment operation. In a short period of time and in perilous circumstances, tens of thousands of personnel had come together to tackle a uniquely challenging event. The destroyed reactor's radiation levels had stabilized, the toxic graphite it had ejected over a wide area had all been removed, and a *China Syndrome*-style meltdown had been avoided. In addition, an exclusion zone had been established and most of the population at risk had been removed to places of greater safety. There was still much more work to do, not least the final 'burial' of the reactor in

The so-called 'biorobots' clearing graphite from the roof.

its concrete sarcophagus, but the containment and clean-up operation was now well in hand. It was time to turn from *what* had happened and investigate *why* it had happened – and *who* was going to be held responsible.

Chapter 4:

THE
INVESTIGATION

Boris Shcherbina had not been in Chernobyl very long before he asked Valery Legasov to begin preparing a report on the causes of the accident.

The scientist already had quite a lot on his plate, trying to formulate responses to the disaster even as it was still happening. But he had quickly emerged from the among the pack of official commission members as someone with acute scientific knowledge, sound judgement and, in Soviet terms, a relatively independent mind. He was a loyal Party man, and remained one throughout the inquiry and afterwards, but he was also more inclined than most of his colleagues to go where the facts took him and not where he assumed Soviet ideology would prefer the investigation to lead.

It should be said that Legasov was tasked only with compiling a technical report, to look at what had failed on the night of the catastrophe and why. The job of deciding who was responsible for this disaster fell to the Kyiv region's Prosecutor's Office, under its chief investigator, Sergei Yankovsky. In the popular imagination, the two investigations have become conflated: Chernobyl's Unit 4 reactor failed because of its inbuilt technical troubles and because the men operating it made terrible mistakes. The big question, as both investigations unfolded, was where the *balance* of responsibility lay – with man or machine? Whether that question was ultimately answered accurately, fairly, or even at all, has been the subject of debate ever since.

Establishing himself initially in Pripyat before the city was abandoned, and then mainly in Moscow, Legasov began to collect documents and data from the power plant and set about interviewing Chernobyl employees, even those confined to hospital beds with life-threatening injuries. Yankovsky, meanwhile, began his criminal probe at a much higher level. Travelling up to Moscow, he made sure that one of the first people he interviewed was Nikolai Dollezhal, the RBMK reactor's chief designer. Yankovsky wanted to familiarize himself with how Soviet nuclear reactors worked and Dollezhal, now well into his 80s and very much a Party grandee, impressed the 30-year-old prosecutor with his knowledge and his analysis of the wonders of his great invention. Yankovsky came away from his audience with Dollezhal firmly believing that RBMK reactors were infallible, and that only human error could make them go wrong. Presumably Dollezhal forgot to mention to

Yankovsky his earlier misgivings about the reactor and the 1979 article he wrote for the journal *Kommunist*, where he openly described how RBMKs could be susceptible to nuclear accidents. It's likely he also forgot to bring up previous RBMK failures, such as the one at the Leningrad Nuclear Power Plant in 1975 (*see* Chapter 1).

From this moment on, the principal control-room actors in the accident – Leonid Toptunov, Aleksandr Akimov, Anatoly Dyatlov – were firmly in Yankovsky's sights, along with the two most senior power plant controllers, Nikolai Fomin and Viktor Bryukhanov. The deaths by radiation poisoning of Toptunov and Akimov just weeks after the explosion removed them from the list of possible indictees. As the inquiries proceeded, new names would be added to the list of those held responsible, but, from the start, Dyatlov, Fomin and Bryukhanov were the big three. Yankovsky was not unaware what was expected of him, though. Wherever his investigation took him – to see Dollezhal, to interview Chernobyl's senior managers and to the factory in the Urals where the Unit 4 reactor's key components were made – Yankovsky was always accompanied by KGB minders, acting as the Soviet state's eyes and ears and making sure the developing 'primarily human error' script was followed.

In theory, Legasov had a freer hand than Yankovsky when putting together his scientific and technical report. But there was one important restriction on his activities: the commission member Shcherbina delegated to oversee Legasov's investigation was Aleksandr Meshkov. This was the deputy director of the Ministry of Medium Machine Building (MMMB), the state department run by the all-powerful Efim Slavsky, the man who more than most had a strong professional interest in seeing Chernobyl's staff held responsible for the Unit 4 reactor explosion. Slavsky had been a champion of ever-bigger RBMK-operated nuclear power stations since the 1960s, and he could not allow them to be seen as faulty or dangerous. This placed him in direct opposition to the Soviet Union's Ministry of Energy, which was more concerned with the day-to-day running of the state's power stations and the operations of its staff. Legasov was left uncomfortably in the middle of these two influential departments: blame the machinery, and incur Slavsky's undying wrath; or put the accident down to human error, and see his career sabotaged by the Ministry of Energy. As we will see, Legasov managed, at much personal cost, to upset both ministries with his conclusions.

As early as 28 April, just two days after the accident, the initial findings were in. Two RBMK reactor specialists had been flown in from Legasov's own Kurchatov Institute of Atomic Energy in Moscow to pore over the logbooks, computer readouts and other data charting the progress of the Unit 4 reactor's demise on the night of the explosion. Their conclusion was, for the time being, satisfyingly vague: 'The cause of the accident was an unruly and uncontrollable power surge in the reactor.' What had caused that surge – human error or a machine malfunction – was left unaddressed. However, for Alexander Kalugin, one of the two Kurchatov Institute experts, the information he looked at rang a distant, and alarming, bell. A year or two previously, Kalugin had been at an RBMK design meeting where a possible manufacturing flaw in the reactor's control rods was discussed. Specifically, it was shown that in very particular circumstances the graphite-tipped rods could become trapped on entry into the reactor, and that this would displace neutron-absorbing water from the reactor and increase reactivity. This had been dismissed

Valery Legasov.

at the meeting as a one-in-a-million eventuality, and it was exactly what had happened at Chernobyl. A troubled Kalugin kept this news to himself. It was much safer for him to wait to see if the information would emerge elsewhere in the investigation. That way, someone else would deliver the bad news to Slavsky and the MMMB, and in the process give an early lead to the Ministry of Energy in the Chernobyl disaster blame game.

To make Legasov and Yankovsky's lives that much more difficult, some of the Soviet Union's prominent politicians rushed to judgement before any official conclusions had yet been reached. 'The accident was caused by a combination of highly improbable technical factors,' pronounced Andranik Petrosyants, the chairman of the Atomic Energy Committee, in a written statement published in the *Los Angeles Times* in early May. 'We are inclined to believe that the personnel made mistakes that complicated the situation,' he added. Petrosyants also promised that a comprehensive report on the disaster would be presented at a conference at the Vienna headquarters of the International Atomic Energy Agency (IAEA), piling even more pressure on Legasov in particular to come to the 'right' conclusions in his investigation. Politburo heavyweight and future Russian president Boris Yeltsin was more direct, telling a German television journalist: 'The cause lies apparently in the subjective realm, in human error.'

With the IAEA conference set for late August, Legasov had four months to prepare his findings – and to navigate a way through the objections and amendments he would certainly be subjected to at the hands of the MMMB, the Ministry of Energy, his fellow commissioners and the Politburo before the report was approved for national and international consumption.

Furthermore, Slavsky's MMMB had lobbied heavily against Legasov being put in charge of the technical and scientific investigation, fearing he was too independent. Legasov was aware of this, and consequently under no illusions that his every move was being monitored by MMMB representatives – if not those of the Ministry of Energy as well.

He had also, some said, been too close to the accident to be able to review it dispassionately. He spent a lot of time at Chernobyl, interviewing scores of its victims in their hospital beds, all the while knowing that many of them would soon be dead, succumbing to their injuries as their irradiated internal organs collapsed and dissolved in the most painful way possible. What's more, he was by now a victim of Chernobyl himself. His skin was darkened by the 'nuclear tan' that afflicted so many of the plant workers and first responders in the hours after the Unit 4 reactor explosion. He was having trouble sleeping and was suffering from nausea and, ominously, digestive troubles. He had been exposed to large amounts of radiation and strongly suspected that it could well have been a fatal, or at least life-shortening, dose.

In that respect, Legasov was a man in a hurry. There is little doubt that his experiences at Chernobyl changed him. He arrived at the power plant a respected, sober-minded scientist and a faithful Party member, yet as his investigation gathered pace he became more and more fixated on what he increasingly saw as his mission. The walls and floors of his two-storey detached villa in Moscow and his office at the Kurchatov Institute, a few hundred metres, away became covered in paper – countless documents and reports relating to the accident that he would read, reread, annotate and analyze obsessively.

On 5 May his investigating committee was ready to deliver its preliminary findings. The trouble was, it was not technically his report to hand over. That was the job of the MMMB-affiliated Aleksandr Meshkov. In addition, Legasov's employer, the Kurchatov Institute of Atomic Energy, was closely tied to the MMMB – and director Anatolii Aleksandrov was one of Efim Slavsky's oldest and closest associates. Whether or how much Legasov was reminded to whom he owed his successful and comfortable career is not clear, but what is undeniable is that his report laid most of the blame for the accident on the men in the Unit 4 reactor control room on 26 April 1986. It was they who had switched off important safety systems prior to the fateful turbine test; they who had instigated the sudden loss of reactor power that initiated the accident; they who had pressed the AZ-5 failsafe button that accelerated the catastrophe. The RBMK's fundamental design flaws were downplayed in the findings. They were not ignored but, whether consciously or unconsciously, Legasov tended to look for human reasons for the disaster where possible.

The preliminary report generally found favour with Slavsky, Aleksandrov and all those in the MMMB camp, but it was not as well received by the rival Ministry of Energy. When its experts read the findings, they simply refused to accept them and advised the Energy Minister, Anatolii Maiorets, not to sign off on the document. Instead, the Ministry of Energy decided to produce its own counter-report, which laid the blame for the Chernobyl accident squarely on the RBMK reactor design. 'Positive void effect' became the rallying cry for Ministry of Energy partisans, who pointed out that this was a feature which affected RBMK reactors and RBMK reactors only. An explosion was bound to happen sooner or later, they argued. The Ministry of Energy report also drew attention to the RBMK's control-rod configuration and composition. Why, it argued, were they tipped in graphite when it was known to be a material that could cause instability in an RBMK reactor?

From here, the departmental feuding intensified. Anatolii Aleksandrov summoned the Interagency Scientific and Technical Council (ISTC) to give its perspective on the accident. Nominally the nuclear power industry's highest authority, and supposedly independent, it was in fact under the control of Slavsky's MMMB. When the council assembled, the meeting was chaired by Aleksandrov himself, who steered its investigations away from technical matters and towards a discussion of the failures of the men in the control room. Efim Slavsky was a glowering presence throughout the ISTC's gatherings, making careful note of anyone who attempted to deviate from the Ministry of Medium Machine Building's official line. When delegates from the state nuclear regulatory agency arrived with design proposals for improving the RBMK's safety, they were denied the opportunity to speak.

In retaliation, the Ministry of Energy went over Slavsky and Aleksandrov's heads and wrote directly to Mikhail Gorbachev, warning him that the two men were attempting to frame the Unit 4 reactor operatives for the disaster and cover up their department's own complicity in the events of 26 April. The letter was composed by Gennady Shasharin, the number two man at the Ministry of Energy, and warned the Soviet leader that accepting only the MMMB's version of events would reflect badly on the state, at a time when Gorbachev was trying to improve the reputation of the USSR internationally. Of course the operatives on the ground made mistakes, Shasharin acknowledged, but that did not absolve the MMMB and its faulty reactor from its share of the blame. For any physicist and engineer looking at the explosion, he argued, it was clear that a 'human error' explanation was not enough. There were technical questions that needed to be addressed: 'Sooner or later they will become known to a broad circle of reactor specialists in our country and abroad.'

This war of words continued for weeks as Legasov digested the responses to his preliminary report and withdrew to put together a final draft. This was completed by the end of June, and on 3 July the principal scientific, bureaucratic and political actors in the drama were gathered in Moscow to hear it presented at a top-level secret meeting, chaired by Mikhail Gorbachev himself.

Shortly after 11 a.m. Boris Shcherbina stood up in the large Kremlin meeting room and presented his commission's findings to the assembled dignitaries. The delegates followed each word of his speech carefully, trying to discern in whose favour it would fall. Both the MMMB and Ministry of Energy camps must have stiffened when Shcherbina announced: 'The accident was the result of severe violations of the maintenance schedule by the operating staff and also of serious design flaws in the reactor.' It seemed for a moment that both sides were to share the responsibility – until, that is, Shcherbina followed up with the qualifying phrase: 'But these causes are not on the same scale.' The next few seconds must have seemed interminable for Slavksy and Aleksandrov on one side and Energy Minister Anatolii Maiorets and his deputy, Shashanov, on the other. Finally, Shcherbina delivered his commission's judgement: 'We find that errors made by the operating personnel in charge were the basic reason for the accident.'

The verdict was in, and the Ministry of Energy had been found guilty. This version of events would be the one presented to the Soviet people and to the wider world from this moment on. But everybody present at the meeting knew that publicly blaming a few individuals for incompetence, or for exceeding their responsibilities, was just a fig leaf. Shcherbina had left them in no doubt about that. RBMK reactors were simply not safe, he told his audience, and his commission recommended that no more be built, unless and until they were brought up to modern operating standards.

As Shcherbina finished his presentation, an angry and confused Mikhail Gorbachev took charge of proceedings. This was the first time since the accident that the facts of Chernobyl had been clearly explained to him from a (relatively) impartial source. For the next few hours he berated those ministers and bureaucrats he held particularly culpable, department by department. First up were Slavsky and Aleksandrov. Although they had both escaped official and public censure for their departments' roles in the catastrophe, the long-serving, octogenarian officials were left in no doubt that the wide-ranging powers they had enjoyed for decades were to be severely curtailed. The two giants of the Soviet nuclear industry were accused of acting like gods, of arrogance and irresponsibility – and of trying to orchestrate a cover-up once the inbuilt technical issues with the RBMK reactor design came to light. 'For thirty years, you told us that everything was perfectly safe,' Gorbachev complained. 'That's the reason why all this happened, why it ended in disaster.'

Slavsky and his deputy at the MMMB, Aleksandr Meshkov, did not go down without a fight. 'The explosion was manmade,' Slavsky argued, pointing out to Gorbachev that the report placed the balance of responsibility for the accident on the operators. Meshkov followed his leader and insisted that, despite what the report said, RBMK reactors were in fact perfectly safe. This was too much for the General Secretary. 'You amaze me,' Gorbachev told him. 'Everything we know about Chernobyl to date leads to one conclusion – the reactor must be condemned. It's dangerous.'

Sensing that Meshkov had gone too far, Energy Minister Anatolii Maiorets played his trump card. 'The reactor is no good,' he began. 'There was a similar accident at the Leningrad nuclear power plant back in 1975. No one ever dealt with it. And the same thing already happened in Chernobyl in 1982... no one learned anything from that accident, either. Foreign sources show that the West has already simulated the Chernobyl accident. Should we continue to lie to the IAEA?' Maiorets's deputy, Gennady Shasharin, joined in. 'The personnel are responsible for the accident,' he announced, 'but its scope, I agree, is in the physics of the reactor.' He followed up by demanding that all RBMK reactors be shut down immediately, until the safety of each one could be demonstrated.

But if Maiorets and Shasharin hoped they had landed the killer blow for their ministry, they were mistaken. If anything, their interventions reminded Gorbachev of the gap between rhetoric and *realpolitik*. Having railed against the irresponsibility of the MMMB and its senior officials, Gorbachev was forced to accept that the Soviet Union was completely committed to its RBMK reactor programme. In private, behind closed doors, the MMMB's leaders could be punished, but the faulty RBMK reactors they had created would be allowed to stay in operation. There was no alternative. Ultimately, Gorbachev was reduced to tinkering around the edges of the problem: asking, for example, if concrete pressure vessels such as the one that had worked so effectively at the Three Mile Incident were the answer. When he was told that they were too expensive to produce and, in any event, did not work with the RBMK reactor design, he was at a loss for words. The Soviet Union was reduced, in effect, to hoping that Chernobyl was a one-off.

Unable to get genuinely impartial information from self-interested parties, such as Slavsky, Aleksandrov and Meshkov on one side and Shashanov and Maiorets on the other, Gorbachev turned increasingly to Valery Legasov for advice. Despite his strong affiliation to the Slavsky-Aleksandrov camp, Legasov tried to answer the Soviet leader's questions as impartially as possible. In the months that had passed since the accident, he had become more and more disillusioned by the political infighting surrounding the accident, while the nuclear industry's general state of unpreparedness for emergencies of any kind had left him profoundly depressed. Asked about the RBMK reactor's qualities when measured against the water-cooled reactors used in other nations, Legasov confirmed to Gorbachev that a country such as the United States would never allow Soviet-style reactors to be built. He also revealed that a 1985 test on a Soviet atomic power station by Finnish experts had been passed only because scientists substituted important Soviet-made reactor components with better-made and more reliable Swedish-American replacements at the last moment.

Such honesty was much appreciated by Gorbachev, but less warmly received elsewhere. For the report he compiled for Shcherbina's commission and for his revelations to Gorbachev, Valery Legasov earned himself the undying enmity of both the MMMB and the Ministry of Energy. Both institutions had long memories, and in the months to come they would have their revenge.

By early evening, after eight hours of debate, Mikhail Gorbachev was ready to wrap up the meeting. The day's findings were summed up in a 25-point plan that outlined how the disaster would be presented, both to the Soviet people and to the outside world; what technical and operational improvements needed to be made to the nuclear power industry; what was to be done to the Chernobyl accident site; and who was to blame for the explosion and what their punishment should be. Because it deliberately failed to address the central issue of the RBMK's design flaws, this plan was compromised from the start. The official line of blaming the plant operators was confirmed, though there would be some acknowledgment of 'problems' with the reactor itself. A similar attempt to have it both ways was enacted at Chernobyl itself: the ruins of the dangerously irradiated Unit 4 reactor were, under Slavsky's direction, to be encased in a protective concrete sarcophagus to supposedly prevent any further leakage of radiation. The rest of the plant, meanwhile, was to be kept operational. This seems irresponsibly reckless in hindsight: to allow workers to return to the site of the world's worst-ever nuclear disaster, now one of the most irradiated places on Earth, and put themselves at huge personal risk. How could it be that 50,000 souls were removed forever from nearby Pripyat while the very epicentre of the catastrophe remained a hive of activity? The short answer is that Chernobyl was too important to close. Hundreds of thousands of people relied on the plant for their electricity; there was no other energy source nearby. Also, mothballing the entire plant would have been an admission that the Chernobyl accident was as bad as the Soviet Union's rivals claimed. That could never be allowed. Instead, thousands of employees would be exposed to dangerous radiation levels on a daily basis for years to come. So important was the power plant that it even outlasted the regime that built it; the governing regime did not close down for good until December 2000 – more than 14 years after the accident and almost 10 years after the collapse of the Soviet Union.

Equally unsatisfying was the decision on who to hold accountable for the explosion. At the head of the list was Viktor Bryukhanov, who was unceremoniously stripped of his Communist Party membership and handed over to Sergei Yankovsky's criminal investigation. Anatoly Dyatlov and Nikolai Fomin were also publicly held to be culpable. On the political front, the most senior officials such as Slavsky, Aleksandrov and Maiorets were all reminded of their important responsibilities but allowed to remain in post. Their deputies were not so fortunate, and Aleksandr Meshkov of the MMMB and Gennady Shasharin of the Ministry of Energy were both sacked. Predictably, the official report following the meeting of 3 July was openly critical of the Ministry of Energy and more guarded in its appraisal of the MMMB: the former was cited for poor management, a lack of training for its operatives and a complacent attitude toward accidents and equipment failures; the latter was mentioned as playing a part in the accident 'due to deficiencies in the construction of the RBMK reactor, which does not fully meet safety demands' – a deliberately foggy comment that neither condemned nor absolved the department of any responsibility. A commitment was made to improve the safety features on the Soviet Union's existing RBMK reactors and, importantly, all plans to build new RBMK reactors were, for the time being, shelved.

The original 'sarcophagus'.

Few attendees at the meeting would have been happy with its outcome. It was clear that the Soviet Union's nuclear industry was in urgent need of a major overhaul, but it was equally obvious that there was neither the institutional will nor the funds to do it. For now, though – and under KGB instruction – everyone involved was told to keep the details of the meeting top secret while Gorbachev's Party leadership team agreed on the best way to frame their decisions to the Soviet people and the international community. It was almost two weeks later, on 19 July, when the state-approved television news programme *Vremya* announced that 'the accident had been caused by a series of gross breaches of the operational regulations of the reactor by workers at the atomic power station... Irresponsibility, negligence, and indiscipline led to grave consequences.' Of the RBMK reactor and its problems, no mention was made.

*

With the Soviet Union's domestic audience formally brought up to date on events, Gorbachev and his Politburo colleagues knew it would be a more difficult task to sell their story to the international community.

In the immediate aftermath of the Chernobyl explosion, Andranik Petrosyants, the chairman of the Atomic Energy Committee, had told the world's media that a full report on the disaster would in time be presented to the International Atomic Energy Agency (IAEA) in Vienna at a specially convened conference. By late August it was time to make good on that promise – and Valery Legasov was the natural choice to share the Soviet Union's findings with the world. Not that it was going to be easy. Instead of a state-controlled media and state-employed scientists, Legasov would be facing a gathering of independent press and television reporters, along with a throng of very inquisitive and sceptical nuclear physicists.

How difficult things would be for Legasov became apparent when he received the IAEA's agenda for the meeting. He was to be allocated just 30 minutes to make his presentation, after which the session would turn into a kind of public hearing on the dangers of Soviet nuclear engineering, for which the verdict had already been decided. The IAEA would call on the Soviet Union to close down all of its RBMK reactors and pay huge amounts in compensation to those nations across Europe affected by radioactive fallout from Chernobyl. Worse still, the IAEA also intended to insist that foreign inspectors be stationed at all Soviet nuclear power stations from now on.

This was unacceptable to the Soviet leadership, and it placed Legasov in a dangerous position. He could not back out of the conference but nor could he make a case to head off the IAEA's ambush without revealing information about Soviet technology that his superiors in the Soviet scientific establishment did not want him to make public. Efim Slavsky in particular was adamant that details of RBMK reactor design should not be shared with 'enemy' nations. His rival Anatolii Maiorets at the Ministry of Energy hit back by pointing out that countries such as the United States were already well aware of how RBMK reactors worked – and much more. The 87-year-old Slavsky, he inferred, was still mired in Stalin-era thinking at a time when the Soviet Union under Mikhail Gorbachev was exploring ways of opening up to the West and cooperating.

With Slavsky and Maiorets squabbling, the Soviet prime minister Nikolai Ryzhkov intervened and told Legasov to include in his report whatever information he felt was necessary, not just on RBMK reactors but on the expected long-term health effects of the explosion, the amount of radiation released during the

10-day reactor fire – and more. Ryzhkov had been profoundly shaken by the disaster and recognized how it had damaged the Soviet Union's standing in the world. He was keen to restore trust and, within reason, to present his state as progressive and willing to learn from its mistakes. Ryzhkov was also a wily political operator and knew that giving Legasov the latitude he needed could work in the Soviets' favour and head off some of the international community's more unreasonable demands. He was correct.

Freed from the shackles of Soviet secrecy, Legasov compiled a wide-ranging presentation that was almost 400 pages long. It drew on the expertise of nuclear engineers, physicists, reactor designers, technicians, medics, and the experiences of Chernobyl employees and operators. As well as a minute-by-minute breakdown of the unfolding disaster, the account included detailed explorations of RBMK reactor construction, Soviet nuclear power planning, and the country's energy strategy. On 25 August at the IAEA's headquarters in the Vienna International Centre, Legasov stood up to begin his presentation – and his 30-minute time slot came and went. One hour turned into two, then three, and still he continued. When he sat down after more than four hours at the podium, the 650 international scientists and journalists in the hall rose as one to give Valery Legasov a standing ovation. The Chernobyl expert's candour had completely won over his audience. They had expected him to recite a short speech full of evasions and half-truths, but instead he had not just delivered an incredibly detailed overview of Soviet nuclear science but had then remained for several hours to answer scores of questions from his peers. 'No one who attended... will soon forget it,' ran a report on

Legasov's speech in the nuclear industry's leading journal, *The Bulletin of Atomic Scientists*. Before his presentation, it reported, 'the conference mood was bleak and tense,' but by the end of the four-day meeting, the atmosphere 'had become cheerful, convivial, verging on the euphoric.'

Overnight, Legasov became a media sensation. Foreign press and television competed to interview him, and internationally renowned physicists queued up to share a few minutes of the Soviet scientist's time. All talk of RBMK reactor closures and IAEA-approved inspectors on Soviet soil was put to one side in the light of Legasov's unprecedented openness.

But what, in reality, had Legasov actually revealed that was not already known? In truth, not much. The world's scientists, media and politicians were so overcome with the excitement of hearing a Soviet insider speak freely and at such length that they neglected to examine too deeply the content of his words. In essence, all Legasov had done was stick closely to the official Politburo-approved line of blaming Chernobyl's Unit 4 reactor operators and soft-pedalling on any criticism of the RBMK reactor and its designers. When asked by a journalist to elaborate on a remark he had made about the Unit 4 reactor's shortcomings, Legasov hastily backtracked, explaining, 'The defect of the system was that the designers did not foresee the awkward and silly actions by the operators.' To pre-empt any follow-up questions, he then revealed that something like half of the Soviet Union's RBMK reactors were currently being upgraded 'to improve their safety'. This appeared to satisfy the reporter's curiosity and Legasov was not pressed any further.

But if Legasov expected a hero's welcome on his return to Moscow after this public relations triumph, he was sadly

Legasov at the Chernobyl post-accident review meeting, 25 August 1986, in Vienna.

mistaken. Bizarrely, he became something of a pariah. Having been told by no less a figure than Nikolai Ryzhkov to be as open as he needed to be in Vienna, he was now informed he had gone too far. 'They understand nothing and even failed to grasp what we managed to accomplish,' a crestfallen Legasov told a colleague after he had been summoned to explain his actions to Party officials.

In truth, Legasov had served his purpose and could now be let go. He had dampened down international unease over Soviet nuclear science and that, for the politicians, was the main thing. 'Since the meeting of member nations of the IAEA, Chernobyl has ceased to be an active element of anti-Soviet propaganda,' Mikhail Gorbachev announced to his Politburo colleagues. If anything, Legasov had become something of an embarrassment to the state, a reminder of its moment of weakness at the IAEA in front of the world's most influential experts and the international media. At the moment of his greatest professional success, Legasov found his career effectively at an end. Within two years, he would be dead (*see* Chapter 5).

After Vienna, as far as the Soviet Union's leaders were concerned, the political and scientific impact of Chernobyl was over. True, some ministerial heads still had to roll, and there were outstanding repairs, improvements and changes to be made to the state's nuclear power stations, but all future housecleaning in those areas would from now on be conducted behind closed doors.

Of course, this would not be the case regarding the criminal cases opened against the men accused of causing the accident. In a legal process that harked back to the Stalinist show trials of the 1930s, the defendants were subjected to a hearing whose outcome had been decided before it had even begun and whose findings would be shared openly with the public.

The hearing's location was strangely symbolic. Soviet law specified that criminal trials had to be held in the closest town or city where the crime itself took place. In this case it should have been Pripyat, but seeing as that city's courtroom was out of use for at least the next 500 years, proceedings were moved to the town of Chernobyl – which, being within the exclusion zone, had also been evacuated but was less radioactive than Pripyat. People could still go there, so long as they didn't stay too long. Once the trial began, on 8 July 1987, an unusual ritual was played out whereby the accused, their lawyers, the prosecutors, judges and court officials were driven to Chernobyl's House of Culture each morning, would spend the day in the former theatre's makeshift courtroom, and then be driven back to where they were staying in a safe area beyond the exclusion zone. This was time-consuming, dangerous – and yet completely logical within the inflexible framework of the Soviet Union's bureaucratic and legalistic system.

The convoy heading into Chernobyl on each of the trial's 18 days brought in the trial's six defendants from the local prison in Ivankiv, 50km (30 miles) away. Of the six, three names were familiar; the other three, less so. As Chernobyl's director, Viktor Bryukhanov was an obvious candidate for prosecution, so it was no surprise that he was one of the first to be charged. Nor was it controversial to see Chernobyl's chief engineer Nikolai Fomin and his deputy Anatoly Dyatlov in the dock. More shocking were the identities of the three remaining defendants. Boris Rogozhkin was Chernobyl's night-shift supervisor and had played no active role in the accident itself. However, Aleksandr Akimov, the night-shift team leader who had played an important part in the accident, was now dead, as was his colleague Leonid Toptunov. Both had succumbed to radiation poisoning, so Rogozhkin was required as a representative of the shop floor. A scapegoat, in other words. Alongside him stood Alexander Kovalenko, the head of the workshop who had signed off on the turbine test, and Yuri Laushkin, Chernobyl's nuclear safety inspector. These three men could feasibly count themselves unlucky to be standing next to Bryukhanov, Fomin and Dyatlov in the courtroom, but the accident was so significant that it needed a sizable number of people from the power plant to be seen to be held responsible.

On the first day of the trial, the presiding judge, Raimond Brize, read aloud the indictment against the six accused. It comprised three violations of Soviet Ukrainian criminal law and included charges of negligence in allowing a dangerous and unsanctioned experiment on the Unit 4 reactor and charges of breaching safety regulations, resulting in the world's worst recorded nuclear accident. Additional lesser indictments of abuse of power and irresponsibility were levelled, to which Bryukhanov and Fomin both pleaded guilty in the hope of earning a lower sentence.

Just 60 people were allowed into Chernobyl's House of Culture to witness the trial, and media coverage was carefully controlled. Journalists from home and abroad were only allowed in on the first day of proceedings, to witness the charges being laid out, and on the final day, when the verdict and sentences were handed down. In between, the world's media was fed a short, and not very detailed, summary of each day's events.

The Ukrainian state prosecutor, Yurii Shadrin, was merciless in his criticism of the defendants, dubbing them 'nuclear hooligans'.

They had failed to control the two men who precipitated the disaster, Aleksandr Akimov and Leonid Toptunov, the former being 'soft and indecisive' and the latter 'a weak specialist'. The expert witnesses called in to testify were all carefully selected to bolster the prosecution case, coming as they did from agencies such as the Kurchatov Institute, which had created the RBMK reactor. When one scientist on the stand began to expound on the intricacies of the positive-void effect – an explanation that would have reflected poorly on the reactor's designers – he was immediately shut down and his testimony terminated. More than 20 written questions for the experts submitted by the defendants were ruled out of order by the judge and rejected. The moving testimonies of two of the explosion's victims were heard, as well as the accounts of 40 different witnesses, including plant employees, police and firefighters. While each statement offered vivid detail about the chaos and confusion at Chernobyl during the accident, they did not provide much technical insight or information as to what was happening inside the Unit 4 reactor control room that night. Instead, the witness testimonies were little more than character criticisms of the defendants. The firefighter Leonid Telyatnikov, for example, when asked what he thought of the men in the dock, replied, 'They should be punished. According to the government commission, it was human error. It was their fault.'

Of the defendants, Bryukhanov was the biggest beast. The man who had built Chernobyl from nothing now stood accused of destroying his creation, of being unable to prevent his employees from carrying out unauthorized tests, and of lying to his superiors over the extent of the accident. His demeanour in court was that of a broken man, ready to accept his fate. Indeed, from the moment he'd been woken in the early hours of 26 April

He got his answer at the meeting of 3 July meeting chaired by Gorbachev: he was thrown out of the Communist Party and handed over to Yankovsky's investigation for questioning. When the news was announced on Soviet television, his mother had a heart attack and died. This may explain why Bryukhanov was in uncharacteristically combative mode when Sergei Yankovsky first came to question him, eager to place the blame for the accident elsewhere. 'Damn it,' he told the investigator, 'I trusted Fomin. I thought it was an electrical test.' This was probably a little disingenuous, but it was also as aggressive as Byukhanov got throughout the whole investigation and trial process. Thereafter he reverted to his old fatalistic self, waiting to accept whatever punishment would be handed down.

Just over a month after having his Party credentials removed, Bryukhanov was formally charged under Article 220, paragraph 2, of the Ukrainian Criminal Code, with 'a breach of safety regulations in explosion-prone plants or facilities'. He was arrested and taken to a KGB detention centre, where he would remain until the trial began, just under a year later.

The legal process, once it began, was something of a relief for at last he would learn his fate. During cross-examination, he told the court that he was satisfied with Chernobyl's safety record up to the point of the accident and claimed that he had not deliberately hidden the extent of the accident from his superiors in the first few important hours after the explosion. Beyond that, he offered little in the way of his own defence. When asked who was responsible for the accident, he named Rogozhkin, Fomin and Dyatlov, but, when pushed, accepted that he was partly responsible too.

Alongside the self-contained Bryukhanov in the dock, Nikolai Fomin cut a very different figure. In March of that year he had tried to kill himself while in custody, breaking his glasses and attempting to cut his wrists. This delayed the trial for several months, and Fomin's fragile mental state, coupled with the lingering effects of the radiation sickness that laid him low in the aftermath of the accident, made him an agitated and distracted figure in court. In rambling and often disconnected testimony, Fomin blamed the accident on Dyatlov and Akimov, and admitted he had not informed Bryukhanov that a turbine test had been approved. He attributed this lapse in judgement to a car accident he had been involved in months before the Chernobyl disaster. It had left him unwell and impaired, he claimed, making him unable to cope with the unrealistically heavy workloads that were imposed on the plant's senior leaders.

Of the three main defendants, Anatoly Dyatlov was by far the most pugnacious – and with good reason. A slew of expert witnesses, as well as his fellow accused, had queued up to name Dyatlov as one of the main instigators of the accident, and of the six defendants on trial he was feeling the most beleagured. He had spent more than six months in hospital, being treated for severe burns and radiation poisoning, and had been discharged only in November 1986. Instead of being allowed to recuperate properly, he was then taken by the KGB and held in custody until the trial began. True to his belligerent nature, the ex-deputy chief engineer came out fighting when state prosecutor Shadrin began his grilling.

Dyatlov's line of attack was that none of the procedural violations which may (or may not) have taken place that night were enough to have caused the accident. It was the RBMK's faulty design that was responsible. In addition, if anyone in the control room was at fault for the Unit 4 reactor problems, it was Toptunov and Akimov. Dyatlov maintained that he was not even in the room when Toptunov accidentally caused the reactor to lose power and when Akimov mistakenly pushed the AZ-5 override button that accelerated the meltdown. This last piece of testimony was contradicted by several other witnesses, but Dyatlov was in full denial mode at this point and even refused to accept that he had directly instructed the control room operatives Aleksandr Kudryavtsev and Viktor Proskuryakov to go to the reactor room to manually insert the broken control rods into Unit 4 reactor, an order that resulted in their deaths.

Fortunately for the authorities, the reporting restrictions placed on the trial meant there was no journalist present to document Dyatlov's criticisms of the RBMK reactor design. They had recognized that Dyatlov would most likely be a difficult defendant, and so it proved. He continually interrupted witnesses and lawyers, disputing evidence and testimony and demanding that he be allowed to submit his own questions to the prosecution team's experts. None of Dyatlov's appraisals of the RBMK's faults made it into the daily news summaries of the trial.

The remaining defendants – Boris Rogozhkin, Alexander Kovalenko and Yuri Laushkin – were more pliable and were consequently given an easier ride. All three pleaded not guilty to the charges against them, but none of them truly expected to be acquitted. It was more a case of hoping they would be given lighter sentences if they cooperated with the prosecution case – after all, the three men had played only bit parts in the catastrophe compared to the lead actors Bryukhanov, Fomin and Dyatlov. By accepting their designated roles, the trio could reasonably expect to resume their careers at some point.

On 29 July a select group of foreign and domestic journalists were invited to attend the final day of the trial, where Judge Brize would deliver his verdict. Unsurprisingly, all six men were found guilty. Yuri Laushkin was handed a prison term of two years, Kovalenko three years and Rogozhkin five years. Bryukhanov, Fomin and Dyatlov were all sentenced to the maximum penalty of 10 years' hard labour. In his summing up, Judge Brize singled out Bryukhanov for particular criticism over his response to the accident: 'Having manifested confusion and cowardice, Bryukhanov did not take measures to limit the scope of the accident, did not implement a plan to protect the personnel and the population from radioactive emissions and, in the information he presented, deliberately minimized the data on radiation levels.' Interestingly, many of the former plant director's old colleagues did not agree with Brize, and 500 signed a petition asking that Bryukhanov be pardoned. It's safe to assume that his old enemy Vasyl Kyzyma was not one of the signatories. Needless to say, the petition was rejected by the Soviet state.

The six defendants all experienced very different fates following the verdicts. Boris Rogozhkin, Alexander Kovalenko and Yuri Laushkin all successfully applied for early release. Within two years of their imprisonment, Rogozhkin and Kovalenko were both working at Chernobyl again. Laushkin would almost certainly have joined them, but he died of stomach cancer soon after gaining his freedom. Nikolai Fomin lasted just one year in jail before being diagnosed in 1988 with 'reactive psychosis', which necessitated his transfer to a state psychiatric hospital. Released from care in 1990, he found employment at the Kalinin nuclear power plant north of Moscow, even though his mental health remained compromised. Anatoly Dyatlov went to prison railing against the injustice of his sentence and, from his cell, carried on a campaign of letter writing, protest and criticism of the RBMK reactor design. Suffering from ill health due to his exposure to radiation, Dyatlov was freed in October 1990. But he did not accept his liberation gratefully; instead he continued to argue against the safety of RBMK reactors, little by little finding an audience prepared to listen to his arguments – especially following the collapse of the Soviet Union at the end of 1991 (*see* Chapter 6). When he died of bone cancer in 1995, Dyatlov had become an unlikely figurehead of the movement to recalibrate the accepted version of the Chernobyl disaster so that men such as Aleksandr Akimov and Leonid Toptunov – and Anatoly Dyatlov – were no longer viewed as the main cause of the accident.

The last of the Chernobyl Six to be freed was Viktor Bryukhanov, who was released on 11 September 1991. As the petition requesting a pardon for him had shown, Bryukhanov was not without friends, and in 1992 a job was found for him at Ukraine's state-owned energy company, Ukrinterenergo, where he continued to work until well into his late 70s. He died in October 2021, aged 85.

By the beginning of August 1987, just 15 months after the Unit 4 reactor explosion, the Chernobyl case was closed. The Shcherbina commission had confirmed the cause of the accident and the trials of Bryukhanov, Fomin, Dyatlov and the other three defendants had seen the guilty parties punished. Now it was time for another form of reckoning to take place: working out the cost – economic and otherwise – of the accident.

Chapter 5:

THE COST

There was a high price to pay for Chernobyl: economically of course, but in other areas too. The environmental consequences were huge and long-lasting, and politically it widened fractures in the Soviet leadership that undermined the fragile edifice of state unity. Factor in the death toll and health impacts at home and abroad, and it's clear that the Unit 4 reactor explosion was among the most expensive accidents of all time.

The Soviet Union was not a wealthy state by the mid-1980s. Apart from a period of rapid industrialization throughout the 1930s, it had never been an economic powerhouse and its experiments with agricultural collectivization, a command economy and centralized planning had all in the end been failures. From the early 1970s, the Soviet economy began to stagnate and by the time of the Chernobyl disaster it was in steep decline.

The attempts to reinvigorate the USSR's economic fortunes through the *perestroika* ('restructuring') policies of the new Soviet leader, Mikhail Gorbachev, had barely got underway when the Unit 4 reactor exploded. The cost of the Chernobyl clean-up – the loss of power-generating capacity, industrial productivity and agricultural land, as well as the ongoing expense of maintaining the accident site – was a drain on the Soviet Union's already meagre resources. Economists disagree whether *perestroika* would ultimately have worked or whether the Soviet Union was already in its death throes, but what's not disputed is that the billions of dollars spent on tackling Chernobyl and its aftermath only made the state's desperate economic situation much worse.

One conservative estimate of Chernobyl's cost for the initial containment and clean-up operation is 18 billion rubles, the equivalent of around $70 billion; another evaluation puts it at $128 billion, which is roughly equal to the entire defence budget for the Soviet Union at that time.

The abandonment of Pripyat and every other town, village and settlement within Chernobyl's exclusion zone saw more than 116,000 people displaced within days of the accident (with a further 220,000 relocated in the coming months). Every single evacuee had to be transported to safe locations and given food, water, clothing and shelter at the state's expense. They then had to be found permanent accommodation and, for the adults, employment. Valentina Bryukhanov, for example, the wife of plant director Viktor Bryukhanov, found herself milking cows on an isolated Ukrainian farm in the days after the disaster. It may not sound like it, but she was one of the lucky ones; unemployment rates among those relocated from the exclusion zone remained high for years after the accident, with farmers and agricultural workers particularly badly affected. Former power plant workers struggled, too. Although Chernobyl remained open and operating until 2000, it was on a reduced capacity and fewer employees were needed to maintain it.

The most ambitious – and costly – response to the human dislocation was to build an entirely new city to replace the one at Pripyat abandoned with such ruthless efficiency. Named Slavutych, it was constructed 45km (28 miles) east of Pripyat. Like Pripyat, Slavutych was an *Atomgrad*, a model city created for the remaining workers of Chernobyl. Its apartments were spacious and its shops well stocked. Slavutych was divided into eight districts, each one created by architects and designers from a different Soviet republic. The Yerevan quarter, for example, was named after the capital of Armenia, and its houses were constructed of the same textured pink stone and in the same style as buildings in that city. Similarly, Slavutych's Baku quarter has a Central Asian feel reminiscent of the Azerbaijan capital, and the Tiblisi quarter is typically Georgian, with many building walls decorated with that state's tradition Bolnisi cross. Workers and materials were shipped in from the eight far-flung republics to build 'their' district, an expensive change from the usual Soviet urban-planning practice of cobbling together prefabricated concrete slabs and hoping they remained upright.

When the time came for the ceremonial opening of Slavutych in October 1988, a last-minute safety check found that its buildings and parks already contained high levels of caesium, plutonium and strontium radiation. However, it was too late in the day to abandon yet another city, especially one that had only just been built, so Slavutych was declared safe for human

An abandoned classroom in Pripyat.

habitation and the first of its 40,000-plus residents moved in – reluctantly at first. Most of those relocated to Slavutych were Chernobyl employees. They knew that living just 45km (28 miles) from the site of the explosion and working at the epicentre of the disaster for the rest of the time was not ideal, but they had little choice. Their skills and employment experience meant many of them were unsuited for other forms of work, certainly not jobs that were as well paid.

While they calculated the unexpected expense of constructing an entire city from scratch, Soviet planners also had to find funds to allow Chernobyl's exclusion zone to be cleared, decontaminated and policed. More than 600,000 workers, known as 'liquidators', were brought in to do this in the weeks and months after the accident. The tasks they were asked to complete left many of them unwell and traumatized: these included exterminating thousands of family pets left behind by evacuees; demolishing and decontaminating entire villages; and cutting down and burying whole swathes of woodland (*see* Chapter 3). When they had finished their work, virtually every piece of equipment used by Chernobyl's liquidators – every truck, armoured vehicle, bus, helicopter, digger, dump truck and crane – was so contaminated they had to be abandoned forever inside the exclusion zone at a cost of tens of millions of dollars.

Then there was the loss of productivity in the factories abandoned within the exclusion zone. Millions of kilowatts of electricity were lost by the destruction of Chernobyl's Unit 4 reactor and the temporary closure of the power plant. Businesses and workshops could not make the things they needed to make without the power provided by Chernobyl's turbine-generated electricity.

As the bills for Chernobyl mounted, individual Soviet states appealed to Moscow for help. Belarus, whose border lay just to the north of Chernobyl, requested $16 billion to fund its clean-up; Ukraine, whose territory bore the brunt of the disaster, appealed for funds too. Officials in the Soviet capital dragged their feet and everybody worked on regardless, hoping that the vast expenses would somehow be met down the line. They never were. The Soviet Union ran out of money and collapsed in economic and political disarray before its accounts could be settled. The Belarus government estimates its economy has lost $235 billion in the more than 35 years since the accident. Up to 7 per cent of government income in Ukraine today is still spent on Chernobyl-related programmes. Across the three most affected nations of Ukraine, Belarus and Russia, more than 7 million citizens still receive benefits in the form of pensions, unemployment payments, disability allowances and healthcare provision for issues connected to the explosion, its clean-up and its aftermath. The total price tag for the disaster to date easily runs into the late hundreds of billions of dollars across Ukraine, Belarus and Russia.

When Chernobyl's Unit 4 reactor exploded in the early hours of 26 April 1986, the mushroom cloud of smoke, ash and graphite particles it released also included a poisonous cocktail of radioactive elements. The iodine-131 emitted in great quantities was deadly but, with a half-life of just eight days, it disintegrated relatively quickly. Of longer-term importance was the caesium-137 that was churned out by the Unit 4 reactor fire. With a half-life of 30 years, it was able to expand its effects across large areas of eastern and northern Europe as the prevailing winds blew up from the south and dispersed it into the atmosphere. Although Ukraine, Belarus and Russia were most affected by Chernobyl's radiation cloud, it spread as far away as Scandinavia, France, the United Kingdom and Ireland in an area covering 200,000km² (77,220 square miles).

In addition to the iodine and caesium radiation, the reactor fire also issued radioactive gases, aerosols and fuel particles, plutonium isotopes and the long-lasting americium-241. Most of the larger, heavier radioactive material fell within 100km (62 miles) of the blast site. Within the most heavily affected areas of Ukraine, Belarus and Russia, the contamination of agricultural land was a significant problem, with both farmland and woodland rendered unusable. A total of 784,320 hectares (1.9 million acres) of highly fertile farmland was removed from production for decades at least. Almost 700,000 hectares (1.7 million acres) of timber-producing woodland were destroyed. Famously, a poisoned area close to Chernobyl became known as the Red Forest, because its dead trees absorbed so much radiation that they turned a bright ginger colour. Hundreds of thousands of contaminated cows, pigs, sheep, goats and chickens were destroyed. Those that survived had to be given expensive fodder treated with radioactive particle binders such as the iron- and salt-based compound Prussian Blue.

The area's waterways were also damaged. Countless fish, amphibious animals and aquatic plants were killed or damaged in the first two weeks after the explosion. Kyiv Reservoir, which supplied the Ukrainian capital city's drinking water, was found to have an unusually high radiation count in the days following the accident. Elsewhere, toxins landed in rivers and lakes, flowing downstream for hundreds of kilometres and leaching into the water table. Irradiated fish were identified as far away as Germany and Sweden.

Regarding the built landscape in the heavily affected exclusion zone, we have already seen in Chapter 3 and above how squadrons of liquidators were sent into abandoned towns and villages to decontaminate buildings with a chemical mixture known as 'water soup', or even to tear down whole settlements in very badly irradiated areas – but this only solved one problem by creating another. The noxious 'water soup' was not collected up by the liquidators but soaked away into the earth; the demolished buildings were not removed but were bulldozed into the ground, where they continued to emit radiation, and probably still do to this day.

Overseas, the radiation cloud drifted across Europe, wherever the wind blew it – mainly to the north and west. In Poland, to the west of Chernobyl, on the morning of 28 April a monitoring station in Mikołajki in the country's northeast registered atmospheric radiation levels 550,000 times higher than the day before. Although the country was a satellite state of the Soviet Union, Poland's government had not yet been briefed by Moscow on the accident; politicians and scientists heard about it only through ambiguous and unverified reports about an accident in Ukraine from BBC radio news bulletins. Acting rapidly, over the next three days, the Polish state administered 18.5 million doses of iodine to its citizens in one of the largest and fastest public health operations in history. Iodine can prevent thyroid cancer in cases of radiation exposure if taken quickly; by contrast, it would be several weeks before the Soviets distributed iodine in any large quantities in its own territory. Poles were warned against foraging for wild foodstuffs such as mushrooms and berries, especially in the east of the country, close to the borders with the Soviet Union states of Ukraine and Belarus.

Significantly, the Chernobyl disaster led to large protests within Poland against its first nuclear power station, then still under construction in Żarnowiec, close to the country's Baltic coast. Although building work continued after the accident, the protests carried on and intensified, and the project was finally abandoned in 1989 when Poland's Soviet-affiliated regime collapsed in the summer of that year.

In Germany, reaction to the accident was, like the nation itself, split down the middle. The country was then divided into the Soviet client state of East Germany and democratic West Germany. In the east, the government did not introduce any public health measures and the state-controlled media was instructed to present what had happened as an 'incident' rather than a full-blown nuclear disaster. 'Experts say: No danger from Chernobyl in East Germany,' declared the East German newspaper *Sächsische Zeitung* – not on its front page, of course, but in a short article buried on Page Six. Television discussion shows allowed East German nuclear experts to tell their viewers that what had happened at Chernobyl took place only because the reactors were old and out of date, whereas East German nuclear reactors were new and faultless, and that what little radiation had been released was not heading East Germany's way.

In West Germany, the disaster was taken more seriously. When heavy rainfall heading up from Ukraine and Belarus dumped large quantities of nuclear material onto Bavaria in southern West Germany, citizens were advised to stay indoors and government warnings were issued telling people to avoid eating salads or wild mushrooms and drinking milk. The country's fledgling Green Party began to organize anti-nuclear rallies under the slogan 'Chernobyl is Everywhere' and saw its popularity rise dramatically, turning it from a fringe group to a major power broker in the country – a status it maintains today. As for Chernobyl's longer-lasting effects, a study by Germany's Institute of Labour Economics in 2018 showed higher rates of long-term cognitive impairment in older people living in areas such as Bavaria, Baden-Württenberg and the old East Germany, where Chernobyl-induced radiation levels in the soil and in the water supply are in some places 500 times higher than the norm.

Further north in Scandinavia, sheep farmers in Norway were forced to destroy their flocks when high levels of radiation were detected in their systems. Even today, Norwegian livestock in many parts of the country are regularly tested for radiation before slaughter. For many years after the accident, and in some places even now, Norwegian and Swedish farm animals in the areas most affected by Chernobyl fallout are not allowed to graze the land or forage but must instead be given specially treated feed. In 2017, 31 years after the disaster, Swedish hunters came across a pack of wild boar with radiation levels 10 times higher than usual. This was directly linked to the irradiation of parts of northern Sweden by Chernobyl fallout, and was particularly attributed to the boars' diet of wild mushrooms, which are able to absorb from infected soil 1,000 times more radiation than other plants and trees.

In the United Kingdom, once the country's excitable tabloid press got hold of the story and began warning readers of the approaching 'death cloud' and the 'nuclear nightmare' that would follow, the emergency services were overwhelmed with phone calls from panicked citizens. As the country's leaders scrambled to put together an official response, the situation turned farcical. In one radio interview, the junior minister for local government, William Waldegrave, mistakenly gave out what he thought was a helpline telephone number but was in fact the number for his department's carpool booking office. When the environment minister Kenneth Baker announced that the radiation risks from Chernobyl were 'insignificant', the head of the National Radiological Protection Board inadvertently contradicted him by publicly warning that the country's death toll would be 'tens of people'.

As public unease mounted, the government soon got on top of things. Nine thousand farms had restrictions imposed in order to stop possibly infected meat and vegetables entering the food chain. Radiation tests were made mandatory in farms in parts of Wales, Cumbria and Northern Ireland, where radiation levels were highest, for 10 years after the accident. A number of medical studies have suggested a link between radiation from Chernobyl and an increase in cases of infant leukaemia, but these are inconclusive. To date, it seems clear that Chernobyl had a larger impact on the food supply than on public health. As in other nations, the British public's faith in nuclear power fell dramatically in the aftermath of the disaster.

Without getting into very technical and hard to understand explanations of exabecquerels, sieverts and curies, the plainest way to describe the amount of radiation ejected into the atmosphere is to compare it to the popular imagination's benchmark for all things nuclear: the Hiroshima atomic bomb. As devastating as Hiroshima's 'Little Boy' bomb was, Chernobyl released at least 400 times more radiation. While this helps to put the event in context, it is also sobering to consider that this massive expulsion of deadly material represented just 3–5 per cent of the Unit 4 reactor's nuclear fuel core. If the reactor fire had spread, lasted longer or the initial explosion been more intense, Chernobyl could have been not so much a disaster as a mass extinction event on a par with the comet that wiped out earth's dinosaurs 65 million years ago.

Like everybody else, the Soviet Union's leaders were caught unawares by Chernobyl. Their response at home and abroad to the accident revealed much about the changes and continuities in Soviet thinking that were pulling apart the state's politics at the time, and which would, in just a few short years, destroy the regime completely, after more than 70 years in power. The political price of Chernobyl was one that the Communist Party ultimately could not pay.

The Soviet Union's leadership under General Secretary Mikhail Gorbachev was inclined to give as little information as possible to its people and the outside world once it learned of the accident at Chernobyl. This was partly out of habit – totalitarian regimes are not characterized by their openness, after all – and partly because the updates they received from Viktor Bryukhanov and other people on the ground in Chernobyl were initially imprecise, if not downright misleading.

As the magnitude of the disaster became clear, the morning after the explosion, the authorities were even more determined to keep what had happened secret. This proved impossible to enforce when Moscow-based foreign journalists began to receive tips from their sources in the Kremlin – vague and unsubstantiated at first, but suggesting that something bad had happened in Ukraine. Lacking specific information, the reporters were unable to publish any stories just yet, but the news found its way back to their national governments, and before long Ukraine's Foreign Ministry in Kyiv was taking calls and receiving visits from overseas diplomats who wanted to know if the rumours they had heard were true. In time-honoured fashion, the Soviets could neither confirm nor deny the allegations put to them – though this became harder to do from 28 April, when Sweden informed the international community of a worrying increase in radiation readings detected in the airstream carried up from Ukraine (*see* Chapter 3). In response, a low-key news item was broadcast on Soviet television that evening, glossing over the accident and downplaying its effects. All this did was to inflame the situation. The international press picked up the story and, denied any factual detail by the Soviets, repackaged it as an impending nuclear apocalypse and led with it on their front pages the next morning.

Even then, Mikhail Gorbachev, the Ukrainian prime minister Oleksandr Liashko and his superior, the Ukrainian premier Volodymyr Shcherbytsky, remained silent. At the time, and until after the collapse of the Soviet Union, this was portrayed as typical of the Communist Party, paranoid about engaging with the West. While this was partly true, there was more to it. Gorbachev had been in power for just over a year when Chernobyl happened. He had not yet fully imposed his plan for a more open and liberal form of politics on the Soviet Union, and the Politburo he chaired was still dominated by hardline Communists from the Stalinist era, such as the former foreign secretary and Party grandee Andrei Gromyko. The traditionalists in the Politburo did not want to share any information about the Soviet Union with its enemies in the West, come what may. The screaming tabloid headlines in Europe and the United States about the accident were proof, the hardliners argued, of anti-Soviet propaganda by an intractable enemy.

Although he was generally in favour of sharing more information with the international community about the accident, Gorbachev could count on the support of only three other Politburo members to back him up: Nikolai Ryzhkov; Eduard Shevardnadze, the future president of Georgia; and Heydar Aliyev, the future president of an independent Azerbaijan. Ranged against them were not just the nine other Politburo traditionalists but the Soviet organs of state, most notably the media censorship department known as *Glavlit*, which had been set up with the creation of the Soviet Union in 1922 and which was not yet capable, either institutionally or operationally, of cooperating with the decadent and bourgeois West.

So instead of doing nothing, Gorbachev and his small group of supporters in the Politburo were actively engaged in trying to win over or outmanoeuvre their conservative colleagues. At the same time, Gorbachev's ally, Nikolai Ryzhkov, was put in charge of a Politburo Operations Group (POG), created to oversee Boris Shcherbina's Chernobyl commission and direct the clean-up and containment programme at the plant. By putting one of his allies in direct control of the Chernobyl response, Gorbachev hoped he would be able to receive more detailed and reliable information on the accident than he had been given so far. He strongly suspected that vital facts were being held back; in setting up the POG, he was trying to take control of the situation.

What this meant in practical terms was that the argument over what to tell the Soviet people and the rest of the world about the accident, as well as what to do about it, raged on behind the Kremlin's closed doors. May Day was approaching and the authorities faced a dilemma. In Socialist states, 1 May is celebrated as International Labour Day, and for most people on the left it is politically the most important date in the calendar. Traditionally, large-scale celebrations, marches and parades took place across the Soviet Union, but there was a powerful argument for calling off festivities in Kyiv: the Ukrainian capital was dangerously close to an accident site where radioactive material was still uncontrollably venting into the atmosphere. But calling off May Day celebrations was like cancelling Christmas (to use a non-Communist analogy). It would have alerted nations outside the Soviet Union that, yes, something truly serious was going on, and it would have sent panic waves through the Ukrainian population. May Day was allowed to go ahead.

On 29 April came further pressure for Gorbachev, when the United States formally offered the Soviet Union medical and technical assistance to help deal with a disaster they were not supposed to know was happening. Despite lacking equipment and resources to deal with the enormous scale of the Unit 4 reactor explosion, the Soviet leader declined. The logic was the same as for the May Day decision: it was more important for the country's leaders to pretend that everything was under control rather than to accept American aid and lose face.

As international speculation mounted, foreign ambassadors were called to a briefing on 30 April at Moscow's Ministry of Foreign Affairs. They were treated to a partial (in every sense of the word) breakdown of casualty numbers and radiation emission figures. Almost as an afterthought, the diplomats were told that, while there was no question that radiation levels were too high, any foreigners living and working close to the accident site would not be prevented from leaving the country if they wanted to – unless, that is, they showed any signs of radiation sickness. In the very unlikely event of that happening, foreign nationals would have to remain in the Soviet Union – for their own safety, of course. The assembled diplomats understood what they were really being told and, after leaving the meeting, immediately advised their compatriots to leave the Soviet Union as quickly as possible. One hundred British students were removed from Kyiv and the Belarus capital, Minsk. A similar number of US and Canadian language students were evacuated from Kyiv. Other nations followed suit. Tourists planning to visit Kyiv that spring cancelled bookings in their thousands; an international bicycle race in the Ukrainian capital went ahead, but only Soviet competitors took part because all the overseas riders pulled out. Still the Soviet leadership refused to provide any concrete evidence on what had happened at Chernobyl – though it did announce it had invited the IAEA director Hans Blix to visit the accident site on behalf of the international community. (This set off a furious debate within the Politburo about what exactly he would be allowed to see and whether it was even safe to let him enter.)

On 5 May the G7 countries of Canada, France, Germany, Italy, Japan, the United Kingdom and the United States issued a statement reminding the Soviet Union of its obligation to inform the international community of any nuclear accidents whose effects would be felt beyond its borders. That same evening, in an effort to regain control of the narrative, the Soviet news agency TASS put out an international press release that gave the most detail so far on the accident and mentioned the reactor fire for the first time. Three days later a small group of foreign reporters was given a managed tour of Chernobyl and, on 9 May, Hans Blix of the IAEA was flown around the accident site by helicopter. This was a risky move by the Soviets, but the reactor fire had been out for days by then and Blix was able to see that things generally appeared to be under control. He was also shown the plans for the concrete sarcophagus designed to entomb the remains of the Unit 4 reactor and, in theory, make it safe. However, the fact that Blix's feet literally did not touch the ground at Chernobyl – he helicoptered in and out without landing – showed that the Soviets were still worried about radiation levels in the area.

For the IAEA's visit, the Soviets had essentially turned Chernobyl into a Potemkin Village. This was the name given to the fake, prefabricated building facades created by the Russian statesman Grigory Potemkin during the reign of Catherine the Great in the late 1700s. They were designed to be moved from place to place while the empress toured the impoverished region of Crimea to convince her that conditions within her realm were much better than they really were. In the early years of the Soviet Union, Vladimir Lenin and Joseph Stalin had both employed a similar concept when they invited left-leaning Western intellectuals, such as H. G. Wells, George Bernard Shaw and Beatrice Webb, to visit the newly established Communist state and housed them in purpose-built and nicely appointed villages populated with well-fed and well-trained happy citizens, each one expertly coached in extolling the virtues of Marxism-Leninism at every opportunity. Not all of these Western visitors bought the lie they were being sold, but some did and wrote in glowing terms about their experiences in the revolutionary state. Lenin, as cynical and calculating a political operator as ever existed, is said to have called such Western sympathizers 'useful idiots'.

Hans Blix was far from fitting this profile, but after his

Chernobyl fly-by, he did hold a press conference in Moscow where he spoke of observing farmers at work in the fields around Chernobyl and watching cars driving up and down busy streets going about their daily business. 'The Russians are confident that they will be able to clean up the area. It will be available for agriculture once again,' he told journalists. He didn't say when.

The Soviets were delighted with Blix's visit and his positive comments. It was a propaganda coup for the state, and a political win for Gorbachev and his moderate allies in the Politburo. On 14 May, 18 days after the Unit 4 reactor explosion, Mikhail Gorbachev at last went public with a televised broadcast across the Soviet Union. He told his fellow citizens how the explosion had taken place and what the authorities were doing to overcome it. He gave reasonably accurate figures for the number of victims so far and even named two of the dead. He did not tell his people everything; even so, his words must have come as a shock to tens of millions of his compatriots who were unused to such candour.

Bringing his audience back to more familiar territory, Gorbachev then spent the rest of his speech attacking the West, which he accused of trying to undermine the Soviet Union in its hour of need. 'The ruling circles of the USA and their most zealous allies... perceived in the event nothing but a further opportunity to raise additional barriers to the development and deepening of the dialogue between East and West, which was already proceeding with difficulty, and to justify the nuclear arms race,' he said in typically convoluted Soviet speak. 'As if that were not enough, an effort was made to show the world that negotiations, to say nothing of agreements, with the USSR are impossible in general, thereby giving the green light to further preparations for war.'

IAEA inspector Hans Blix at a press conference in Moscow in May 1986.

The Soviet leader was trying to have it both ways – or three ways, even – in his speech. He attempted to win over his fellow citizens by talking to them directly, the international community by talking honestly, and the hardliners by attacking the West. Sadly, Gorbachev's announcement was a failure on every front. The Soviet people were simply not programmed to accept such openness from their political masters. What they heard in effect was a tale of danger and failure on their leader's watch. Mikhail Gorbachev was never a popular leader in his home country, and this broadcast helps explain why. For his whole time in power, he spoke a political language that his compatriots did not understand. Equally unsatisfied was the international community, which viewed Gorbachev's anti-Western diatribe as unnecessary and unhelpful. Many foreign leaders understood that his allegations were designed for domestic political consumption, but felt they could not be allowed to pass. Diplomatic relations between East and West frosted over again after the honeymoon period of Gorbachev's first year in power. Finally, the grim old men of the Politburo, who longed for a return to the days of ideological purity and strong, Stalin-style leadership, regarded Gorbachev's tough-talking as hollow words and his admission of trouble at Chernobyl as a sign of weakness.

In time, Gorbachev would mend fences with the international community but he would never come to terms with his rivals at the traditionalist end of the Communist Party or with most citizens of the Soviet Union.

The final category to consider when looking at the Chernobyl disaster is the most important one: the human cost.

The first victim of Chernobyl was Valery Khodemchuk, who

had been in the pump room next to the Unit 4 reactor when it exploded and whose body was never found. He was followed by Vladimir Shashenok, an engineer crushed under a pile of debris in one of the offices destroyed by the blast. Given the severity of the explosion, it is miraculous that these were the only two people to die on the night of the accident itself. If the disastrous turbine test had taken place during the day as originally planned, the death toll would surely have been much higher.

Of the hundreds of police, military, firefighters, medics and plant operatives who battled the blaze and helped to contain the accident site, 28 would die in the following weeks and months of acute radiation syndrome (ARS). Having been exposed to fatally high levels of radiation, they all succumbed to their illnesses in horrible ways. The effects of radiation exposure are felt within minutes: nausea and vomiting, followed by diarrhoea, headache and fever. Depending on how or where individuals were exposed, they are also likely to suffer burns and lesions. These initial symptoms will be followed an hour or two later by dizziness, disorientation and fatigue. Once a patient is hospitalized, it will be only a matter of time before they begin to cough up bloody vomit and suffer uncontrolled internal bleeding. Such was the fate of the Unit 4 control room operatives Aleksandr Akimov and Leonid Toptunov. The former passed away on 11 May, 15 days after the explosion; the latter followed him three days later. Akimov was 33 years old, Toptunov just 25.

In the next few weeks, a further 134 of Chernobyl's first responders would be diagnosed with ARS. They would survive, or at least not die within a year or two of the accident, but most would be left with debilitating injuries and conditions. Between 1987 and 1994, when records stopped being taken, a further 19 more people involved in the explosion died from a variety of causes – excluding accidents – in which exposure to radiation may have played a part.

Three days after the Unit 4 reactor meltdown, the KGB began keeping records of the number of hospital admissions across Ukraine for people with radiation sickness. On 28 April it was 54, and by 3 May, 911. One day later this had risen to 1,345. It was clear within a week of the explosion that its effects had spread well beyond those directly involved in the accident; hundreds of children were admitted to hospital with radiation sickness, some from as far away as Kyiv.

The further in distance and time we move from the accident, the more difficult it becomes to directly attribute deaths and health problems to Chernobyl. It's estimated that as many as 20,000 thyroid cancer cases have come about as a result of the accident, mainly in the Ukraine-Belarus region but as far afield as Scandinavia too. This high number is in part due to the delay in distributing cancer-preventing iodine to populations in the most severely radiation-affected areas. It is harder to assess the number of deaths and severe health problems that were secondary effects of Chernobyl – the weakened immune systems, organ failures and bone problems that exposure to radiation can exacerbate, not to mention the mental-health issues, depressions, substance abuse and alcohol addictions that followed in the wake of the disaster. Post-traumatic stress disorder (PTSD) was not a condition widely recognized at that time, especially in the Soviet Union, but it is reasonable to assume that several hundred of those associated with Chernobyl and its aftermath experienced PTSD in some degree or other.

*

One high-profile victim of Chernobyl worth looking at in some detail is Valery Legasov, a man who experienced the pain of radiation exposure, the PTSD of being centrally involved in a major tragedy and, finally, the depression linked to the difficulties of dealing with emotionally challenging events.

Few people worked harder trying to contain the accident at Chernobyl and to understand its causes and consequence afterwards than the Shcherbina commission's lead scientific representative. From the moment he arrived in Chernobyl, the morning after the accident, Legasov put himself in harm's way with little regard for his own health. He understood immediately that his role could not be carried out without exposing himself to life-threatening amounts of radiation. In the crucial first day or two after the accident, he made several important contributions to the clean-up and containment process, but it's for the one questionable call he made that he is best remembered – and most vilified. Legasov's suggestion that the best way to put out the Unit 4 reactor fire was by burying it in sand, lead and boron seemed perfectly feasible at the time, and there were few viable suggestions from other people, but it soon became clear that it would lead only to further – and possibly worse – problems. Several helicopter crewmen who were charged with dumping the material onto the reactor suffered major health problems and even death because of the operation, which weighed heavily on Legasov's conscience ever after. Furthermore, although the fire was eventually extinguished, the dumped material caused the remaining nuclear fuel to begin reacting again and the weight of the congealed and irradiated sand, lead and boron mixture almost initiated another, worse meltdown (*see* Chapter 3). Legasov's colleagues and rivals used this as a stick to beat him with constantly. He was only a chemist, after all, they said; how could a non-physicist be put in charge of such an important event, they asked.

He further alienated powerful figures in his industry by first pinning too much of the blame for Chernobyl on the Ministry of Energy at a key meeting with Mikhail Gorbachev, and then upsetting his own patrons in the Ministry of Medium Machine Building by revealing too many of its inner workings to the outside world at the IAEA conference in August 1986. As a result, Legasov found himself an isolated figure. The following month, on his fiftieth birthday, there was an expectation that the Soviet leadership would reward him for his leading role in the Chernobyl containment operation and its aftermath. It was touted that he would be given an award – either a Hero of the Soviet Union award or Hero of Socialist Labour, his state's two most prestigious medals. Instead, he was presented with a watch – and a not particularly valuable, Soviet-made watch at that. This was the first public sign that he was falling out of favour.

Just a few weeks later, Anatolii Aleksandrov, the 83-year-old, nuclear industry power broker, announced he was retiring as both president of the Soviet Academy of Sciences and director of the Kurchatov Institute. Ordinarily, Legasov would have stepped into his shoes at the Kurchatov: he was the de facto leader of the institute anyway, and Alexandrov more of a ceremonial head. But in another very public snub, Legasov was passed over by his colleagues, who believed he had betrayed them at the IAEA Vienna conference.

It was around this time that the effects of his exposure to radiation at Chernobyl began to take its toll. The telltale signs of acute radiation sickness began to manifest themselves:

headaches, nausea, exhaustion. His white blood cell count increased, indicating possible leukaemia or radiation-induced cancer. By May 1987, with his health deteriorating and his spirits low due to his professional troubles, Legasov took an overdose of sleeping pills while being treated for radiation sickness in hospital. He survived, and decided afterwards to dedicate himself to campaigning for better RBMK safety standards in the Soviet nuclear power industry – a move that helped him lose what little support he had left among his colleagues. In the autumn of 1987 he had to endure yet another humiliation, when a decision to give him the Hero of Socialist Labour award was finally announced and then withdrawn at the last moment following objections from staff at the Kurchatov Institute. This appeared to be not just cruel but vindictive.

After this, Legasov's behaviour began to change. He knew that his illness meant he had little time left and that his scientific career and reputation had been irreversibly tarnished by what looked to be an organized campaign against him. He began to make tape recordings of his increasingly critical thoughts on the nuclear power industry's safety standards and on the direction the Soviet Union was taking under Mikhail Gorbachev.

On 26 April 1988, two years to the day after the Chernobyl disaster, Legasov submitted a proposal to the Kurchatov Institute suggesting that more cooperation between different agencies involved in nuclear power generation would make the industry safer. It was rejected. The following morning, after his wife had left the family home to go to work, Legasov hanged himself in his living room. He left no suicide note. There was no need. He knew that his declining health was only the preface to a prolonged and painful death. He was also burdened by guilt over some of

Chapter 6:
COLLAPSE

The Soviet Union did not collapse because of Chernobyl, but the accident did offer a very large helping hand. It was already in trouble by 1986, locked in a cripplingly expensive arms race against the United States which it could not afford and could never win. The state was, according to the *Daily Telegraph*'s Moscow correspondent at the time, 'Upper Volta with rockets'. This was hyperbole, but only just; the Soviet Union was broke.

From the creation of the Soviet Union in 1922, the state's economy operated on a permanent war footing, whether it was engaged in conflict or preparing for it. A damaging civil war after the Russian Revolution of 1917 was followed by a wary coexistence with the rest of the world. Under Joseph Stalin, who led the state from 1924 until his death in 1953, the Soviet Union dedicated all of its resources to making itself industrially and militarily powerful to protect the revolution from the threat of fascism in the 1920s and 1930s, and from the capitalist West after World War II. This led to something of a paradox, as the state discovered the only way it could destroy the West militarily was to trade with it economically. For decades the state-owned industries produced a range of goods for export, including weapons, industrial plant machinery, oil, gas, agricultural goods, metals and minerals. Most of the revenue raised from foreign sales was ploughed back into maintaining the country's military might, with a consequent lack of investment in all other areas of society. Public housing was substandard; healthcare basic at best. Citizens would routinely queue for hours outside grocery shops with empty shelves so that the state's armed forces could be kept supplied with weapons.

After he took power, Stalin introduced a programme of rapid industrialization to kick-start the Soviet economy, which had the capitalist West worried at a time when the United States and Europe were in the depths of the Great Depression. But before long reality began to bite, as Stalin's command system of enforced quotas and production targets was shown to be unworkable. The typical Soviet factory went from being a hive of activity to a hotbed of corruption, waste, malingering and inefficiency. Factory managers routinely falsified their manufacturing figures, and many of the goods produced then disappeared into the state's black economy. To add insult to injury, a similar attempt by Stalin to industrialize agricultural production in the 1930s was even more disastrous and resulted in the decimation of Soviet farming and millions of deaths by famine (*see* Chapter 1).

By the end of the 1930s, the Soviet Union was on the edge of a precipice. As with many other nations, it was World War II that revived the Soviet economy. From the moment German forces invaded the Soviet Union in Operation Barbarossa in June 1941, the USSR's factories began to operate at full capacity through to the end of the war, working non-stop to manufacture arms, ammunition, tanks, planes and ships in huge numbers. By most estimates the Soviets built more than twice as many tanks in the war as the Germans, for example.

The end of hostilities in 1945 presented the Soviets with an expensive and existential new problem. The nuclear bombs dropped by the United States on the Japanese cities of Hiroshima and Nagasaki on 6 and 9 August 1945 saw the birth of the Atomic Age, and the Soviet Union from that moment on was playing catch-up to find both the funds and the technical expertise to match the Americans in the arms race that followed. With characteristic ruthlessness, Stalin quickly turned the Soviet Union into a nuclear power. Having learned in the early 1940s that the Americans were attempting to create an atomic superweapon, he appointed the physicist Igor Kurchatov in 1943 to oversee the state's nuclear bomb programme. On 29 August 1949 the Soviets exploded their first nuclear device, known as RDS-1, or First Lightning, at its Semipalatinsk Test Site in Kazakhstan. One of Kurchatov's colleagues on the project was Nikolai Dollezhal. He would go on to invent the RBMK nuclear reactor and become one of the leading lights in the Ministry of Medium Machine Building, which was set up in 1953 to oversee the Soviet atomic weapons and energy programmes – including the building of Chernobyl.

There's no good time to experience a catastrophic nuclear disaster, but for the Soviet Union the spring of 1986 was a particularly difficult moment. Stalin's death in 1953 had seen the relatively liberal Nikita Khrushchev take charge of the Soviet Union. He released many political prisoners, took a pragmatic rather than ideological approach to leadership and, most famously, openly denounced to his Party colleagues the revered Stalin as a repressive and harmful figure in Soviet history. None of this sat well with his more conservative comrades, who colluded against Khrushchev in secret and began hatching plans to bring him down. Their moment came with the Cuban Missile Crisis of October 1962, when the Soviets tried to install atomic bombs on the Caribbean island but were forced by the Americans to back down. For several days the world stood on the brink of war as US Navy warships prevented Soviet ships carrying nuclear warheads from landing on Cuba. Khrushchev blinked first and ordered his vessels home – and his fate was sealed. One year later he was deposed, replaced by the more hardline Leonid Brezhnev.

Under its new leader the Soviet Union introduced the so-called Brezhnev Doctrine, asserting its sphere of influence over the whole of Eastern Europe. This meant using force where necessary to put down dissent against Communist rule, as in Czechoslovakia in 1968, and deliberately cooling relations with the United States and the West. A happy financial windfall in the early 1970s gave the Soviets the confidence to do this and to present itself as a genuine equal to the US military machine. In 1973 the world's energy markets were thrown into turmoil after OPEC (Organization of Petroleum Exporting Countries) deliberately restricted oil and gas production. Dominated by Saudi Arabia and with members including Iran, Iraq, Kuwait and Libya, OPEC was acting in retaliation for the West's support for Israel in the Arab-Israeli Yom Kippur War of October that year.

With oil and gas in short supply, prices soared by up to 300 per cent and producers who were not members of OPEC, including the Soviet Union, cashed in, charging $12 a barrel for oil that had been just $3 before the crisis. Enjoying its unexpected cash bonus, the Soviet Union began very publically to build up its stores of nuclear weapons, making sure the Americans were aware of what they were doing.

The Soviets couldn't be too open about their bomb-making programme, however. They claimed to have thousands of nuclear warheads in their armoury, though in reality the true figure at that time was more like hundreds. This was still enough to destroy the world many times over, but pretending to have a larger arsenal than they did made the Soviets appear more powerful, ensuring the West didn't try anything too confrontational and that the Cold War did not turn hot. Surprisingly, this fitted in with the Americans' global agenda, too – or at least some elements within the United States. For many years the CIA and other national security organizations purposely overstated to America's presidents their estimates of Soviet nuclear capabilities. This ensured that the interests of what was known as the national security state remained at the forefront of American political life, with its budgets protected and its power to operate around the world with impunity unchecked. It also kept America's arms manufacturers busy with lucrative weapons contracts.

But by the end of the 1970s this trope of two evenly matched foes was beginning to wear thin. The Soviet Union was struggling to keep up – and this was starting to show. Global fuel prices had stabilized, meaning that revenues from the sales of Soviet oil and gas began to fall. Brezhnev, never the most dynamic leader, was old and ill, and the Soviet Politburo was populated with equally ageing and backward-looking hardliners queuing to replace him. On Christmas Eve, 1979, Soviet forces invaded Afghanistan in what was supposed to be a quick in-and-out operation to install the pro-Moscow People's Democratic Party of Afghanistan (PDPA) as the government of the troubled state along the Soviet Union's southern border. This quickly turned into a messy, drawn-out and expensive war, which highlighted the Soviet Union's weaknesses to the rest of the world. Far from showing itself as an implacable nuclear global power, it now seemed to be a military lightweight, unable to defeat Afghanistan's poorly armed and loosely organized guerrilla forces known as the mujahideen.

Brezhnev's death in 1982 saw the Soviet Union at a crossroads. Should the power brokers in the Kremlin go for more of the same when choosing their new leader? Or should they opt for change, in the same way that voters in the United States and United Kingdom, for example, had recently done by electing the ideologically driven radicals Ronald Reagan and Margaret Thatcher as president and prime minister respectively.

At first, the kingmakers in the Politburo played it safe, installing the 68-year-old former KGB director Yuri Andropov as the new general secretary in November 1982. As if on cue, he fell terminally ill just two months later and spent the last half of his 14-months tenure in a Moscow hospital bed. He was replaced by the equally short-lived Konstantin Chernenko, whose poor health, vacant expression and zombie-like demeanour in the few public appearances he made in his year in office led satirists to joke that the Politburo had taken Soviet ideology to its logical conclusion and had the head of state embalmed while he was still alive.

Chernenko's death on 10 March 1985 was not unexpected, and plans were already in place to anoint his successor. Just 24 hours later, 54-year-old Mikhail Gorbachev entered office as the General Secretary of the Communist Party of the Soviet Union. This was a new departure for the Soviets, and not everybody within the Party hierarchy agreed with the appointment. For some, Gorbachev was too inexperienced; for others, too radical. Before becoming Soviet leader, he had publicly spoken of the need for change, for economic reform and a more liberal, open society. By the 1980s the people of the Soviet Union had been conditioned to accept one-party, authoritarian rule; except for the state's oldest citizens, it was the only form of government anybody knew. Gorbachev's proposals to allow some entrepreneurs to set up their own businesses, for example, worried citizens who were used to the state providing for all of their needs, or at least attempting to do so. On the other hand, there were those – admittedly smaller in number – who saw in Mikhail Gorbachev someone who would improve their lives and allow them to be more free.

This split in society was reflected among the state's politicians and military leaders. A smaller, younger cadre supported Gorbachev. These were men like Nikolai Ryzhkov, Eduard Shevardnadze and Boris Yeltsin, all of whom would go on to have successful careers once the Soviet Union was dissolved. Opposing them, as soon as the scope of Gorbachev's ambitions for the nation became clear, were old-timers such as the influential former foreign secretary Andrei Gromyko; the soon-to-be KGB head Vladimir Kryuchkov; the Red Army general Dimitry Yazov; and younger conservatives like Gennady Yanayev, future vice-president, and Oleg Baklanov, in charge of the Ministry of General Machine Building, which controlled the Soviet Union's space exploration programme. Throughout Gorbachev's time in power the two sides would look to score points off each other, keen to capitalize on mistakes and missteps that could be used either to boost or to hold back the cause of reform. When the Chernobyl accident happened, just over a year into Gorbachev's reign, the official reaction to it would in large part be conditioned by these political divisions, a response that would help to further undermine an already weak Soviet state.

Internationally, the accession of Mikhail Gorbachev was greeted with cautious optimism. US president Ronald Reagan had famously called the Soviet Union an 'evil empire' in 1983, but he and his advisors softened their stance when they saw that Gorbachev wanted to end the Cold War and build better relationships with the outside world. Britain's prime minister, Margaret Thatcher, approved of him, too, telling the BBC: 'I like Mr Gorbachev. We can do business together.'

Yet in the mid-1980s business in the Soviet Union was not good. Most of the state's earnings came from foreign oil and gas sales. These were fairly stable through most of the 1970s, and by the end of that decade they accounted for more than 30 per cent of the Soviet Union's income. But from the mid-1980s that started to change. At precisely the moment when the Soviets needed to fund the ongoing invasion of Afghanistan, Saudi Arabia tore up the international agreements it had made to keep oil production steady, and in the autumn of 1985 began to flood the market with cheap crude. Its reasons for doing this were complex, motivated in part by a desire to keep rival OPEC producers in check and maintain the Saudis' control of that organization. The result, for the Soviet Union at least, was that its oil and gas revenues fell dramatically, by more than half. The state was still trying to make good its losses in spring the following year when the

Mikhail Gorbachev.

Unit 4 reactor at Chernobyl blew up. It is estimated that in 1986 the Soviet economy lost $20 billion in revenue, largely due to lower oil and gas prices. With reduced oil revenues coming in, the Soviet Union was forced to borrow more from international markets: $20 billion in 1986, rising to $50 billion in 1989. Even before Chernobyl, the Soviet Union was running on empty; after Chernobyl, it ground to a halt.

While the men in Moscow's finance ministry worked out how to pay for the disaster at Chernobyl, Mikhail Gorbachev and his Politburo colleagues were falling out over how – or whether – to explain it to the Soviet people and the outside world. This widened existing splits in the Soviet hierarchy, forcing some politicians further to the extremes and, ultimately, towards the removal of Gorbachev from power.

'The more honest we are, the better,' Gorbachev told his colleagues at the first full Politburo meeting after the accident, on 1 May, going on to say that they should tell the leaders of the Eastern Bloc countries what had happened, as well as the governments in Washington DC and the major European capitals. Not surprisingly, his ministers were divided on the issue. Some agreed with him, on either moral or practical grounds: it was the right thing to do, and besides, as they pointed out, US spy satellites and surveillance aircraft had surely photographed the accident site already anyway. Deny everything, others argued; grainy high-altitude photographs prove nothing. Caught in the middle, Gorbachev dithered. For a new and inexperienced leader, establishing his reputation meant everything. In the absence of hard news in the days after the explosion, rumours about what had happened at Chernobyl were rife, and foreign heads of state were taking a dimmer view of the Soviet general secretary with every passing day that he remained silent.

When Gorbachev finally spoke in public about the accident, with his television broadcast of 14 May (*see* Chapter 5), he spent as much time on screen attacking Western governments and their media outlets for their misrepresentations of the disaster as he did explaining to his fellow citizens what had happened at Chernobyl. This won him few friends in Washington, London, Paris and Bonn, but there was method in Gorbachev's madness. As a new leader, he had not yet established his full authority over the Politburo, and he needed to appease his more conservative colleagues with traditional anti-capitalist rhetoric until he was sure his position was secure. The foreign leaders he could deal with later, and it was indeed the case that Gorbachev would soon win back the international support he lost that day. In fact, for the rest of his reign he continued to be more popular overseas than he was at home, his visits abroad inciting pop-star-style outbreaks of 'Gorbymania' among excited crowds which his public appearances at home came nowhere close to replicating.

What Gorbachev thought would get the Soviet people singing his praises were the *glasnost* policies he was slowly beginning to roll out. These included relaxing the state's control of the media, allowing journalists to report fairly openly on the Chernobyl disaster and its aftermath. Gorbachev's intentions may have been honourable, but this was a risky undertaking. The Soviet people were not used to hearing bad news about their own nation and they did not always appreciate what they were now being told. To many people, what they heard sounded like an admission that their leader had failed them. Gorbachev's hardline political opponents were unhappy, too, thinking that in their liberalizing general secretary they had another Khrushchev on their hands. For them, Chernobyl was Gorbachev's Cuban Missile Crisis.

Away from Moscow, Gorbachev and his Politburo allies struggled to find support among Ukraine's political leaders. Traditionally, Russia was the true seat of Soviet power and all other regions deferred to it. Even the fact that the Soviet Union's three longest-lasting leaders were Georgian (Stalin) and Ukrainian (Khrushchev and Brezhnev) did not alter this fact. After the accident at Chernobyl, Moscow-based political leaders were quick to blame the 'yokels' and 'rednecks' down in Kyiv for it, inferring that it was all that could be expected from a bunch of provincial hayseeds. Gorbachev himself did not help matters when, just days after the Unit 4 reactor exploded and while it was still pouring radioactive material into the atmosphere by the tonne, he insisted the traditional open-air May Day parade go ahead in Kyiv. This set him in direct opposition to the Ukrainian Communist Party leader Volodymyr Shcherbytsky, who wanted it called off in the interests of public safety. It's not known how many innocent Ukrainian citizens died or suffered illness or disease after attending the 1986 May Day parade in Kyiv, but Gorbachev's insistence it go ahead remains one of his most controversial decisions. Certainly, Shcherbytsky never forgave him, and the two men became bitter enemies ever after. Gorbachev's popularity in Ukraine declined even further thanks to his continued refusal to visit Chernobyl. It would be almost three years – in February 1989 – before he finally made it to the accident site, by which time it was already too late to save his political skin.

Another sign that Moscow in particular and Russia in general was regarded as more important than the rest of the Soviet Union was the initiation of Operation Cyclone, 48 hours after the Chernobyl accident. When the Soviet Ministry of Meteorology looked at its weather forecasts for the days following 26 April, it saw that the prevailing winds were due to push the radioactive dust cloud from Chernobyl up through Russia and towards Moscow. Rather than allow this to happen, the Soviet minister for hydrometeorology, Yuri Izrael, devised a plan whereby the toxic mass of air would be intercepted long before it reached the Soviet capital. A fleet of Tu-16 bombers was loaded with modified artillery shells, each one filled with silver iodide, and sent off on a very unusual raid. Tracking the Chernobyl cloud, the Tu-16 bombers intercepted it over Belarus and fired their silver iodide-filled missiles into it. Silver iodide has a similar structure to ice crystals, and the purpose of launching it into the cloud was to encourage water droplets to cluster around each silver iodide particle and make them fall as precipitation. In short, Moscow deliberately caused millions of litres of radioactive rain to fall on the people of Belarus so that it would not fall on the citizens of Russia.

Operation Cyclone was a top-secret undertaking. This was fortunate for Mikhail Gorbachev, who was already feeling the heat from the international community, his conservative opponents, an antagonistic leadership in Ukraine and an, at best, bemused Soviet public. The last thing he needed to be made public were details of what was the equivalent of a poison-gas attack on the people of Belarus.

While Chernobyl certainly undermined the Soviet Union from within, it also assailed it from without. It's possible to draw a direct line from the accident to the growth of green and environmental organizations across Europe, and then on to the

A Tupolev Tu-16 bomber. Aircraft like this one were modified to deliver a payload of silver iodide-filled missiles, which were employed above Belarus, causing radioactive rainfall.

pro-democracy and independence movements that proliferated throughout the Eastern Bloc and into the Soviet Union itself.

Environmentalism did not begin with Chernobyl. In West Germany, the Green Party (*Die Grünen*) was founded in 1980 but it was only after the accident that it began to take off, winning an 8.3 per cent share of the vote in the 1987 federal elections. Not surprisingly, support for the Greens was highest around each of West Germany's 18 operational nuclear power stations and 14 plants that were then under construction. When plans were drawn up for a new nuclear power plant in Bavaria in the late 1980s, a petition launched to prevent it gathered 900,000 signatures.

Across the border in East Germany, the environmental and anti-nuclear power movement was by necessity more secretive.

It had formed in the late 1960s and at first was made up mostly of hippies and other countercultural dropouts, men and women who were retreating from state control rather than confronting it, and whose focus was on peace, ending world poverty, women's and minority issues, and self-sufficiency. This began to change after Chernobyl, when the anti-nuclear power movement gained hundreds and then thousands of new recruits. Unlike in West Germany, where much of the growth of anti-nuclear power dissent could be described as yet another example of NIMBYism and was very locally based, the East German protest was spread across the country and had a wider, international dimension. East German activists sought out links with other anti-nuclear groups in Poland, Czechoslovakia and other Eastern Bloc countries, as well as with environmental organizations in Western Europe. This political engagement inevitably became tied in with other issues affecting nations behind the Iron Curtain: the lack of political freedom, the too-strict social controls, one-party Communist rule and, ultimately, the hegemonic rule of the Soviet Union across the entire region.

A similar movement grew up in Poland. This was in addition to the trade union Solidarity, which had been formed in 1980 to fight for greater workers' rights and which quickly became a thorn in the flesh of the country's repressive government. Solidarity paved the way for the anti-nuclear and environmental movements in Poland as it showed that, in the last analysis, the state did not have the political will or the power to fully crack down on well-organized protest. Starting life as a group opposed to forced army conscription, Poland's Freedom and Peace organization took up the cause of environmentalism after Chernobyl and saw its membership expand rapidly. In January 1987 Freedom and Peace staged a public demonstration in Wrocław, in western Poland, protesting against a large metal works in the city that was known to be polluting the air and water supply locally. Although the police broke up the demonstration and made several arrests, the area's political leaders announced just weeks later that the plant would be phased out within the next five years.

Solidarity itself endorsed Freedom and Peace's protest, understanding that this form of dissent was another route to undermining the country's unpopular Communist regime. 'The environment is one of the issues, like housing or health, that could cause a social explosion in Poland,' Wladyslaw Frasyniuk, Solidarity's leader in Wrocław, told the *Washington Post*. 'We have to find ways to focus people's energies on problems like this that touch their lives and which can be affected by social pressure.' In response, Poland's government set up something called the Environmental Protection Commission, to show its citizens it was paying attention to their post-Chernobyl concerns. It failed to convince many Poles of its good intentions, though. As in East Germany, the anti-nuclear and environmental anxieties thrown up by Chernobyl became wrapped up in other issues that drew in more and more supporters and chipped away at the state's authority. This was not good news for political leaders in East Germany, Poland and the rest of the Eastern Bloc, but they were not overly concerned so long as they were backed up by the might of the Soviet Union if things got too out of hand. But that was about to change, too – in part because of what had happened at Chernobyl.

In Ukraine, many people were unhappy, not just about the Chernobyl accident itself but by the state's response. Everybody understood that it was Moscow – and therefore Russia – where the big decisions affecting Ukrainian people's lives were made. There were grumblings after the disaster that, of course, Moscow would place its faulty nuclear reactors on Ukrainian soil rather than in Russia, and that Mikhail Gorbachev would make sure he stayed safe in the Soviet capital and not show his face anywhere near the accident site. This conveniently ignored the fact that the Chernobyl nuclear power station was the brainchild of the Ukrainian nuclear experts Efim Slavsky and Anatolii Aleksandrov, had been authorized by the Ukrainian-born Soviet leader Nikita Khrushchev, and that its problematic RBMK reactors had been designed by the Ukrainian nuclear physicist Nikolai Dollezhal. The political atmosphere in Kyiv in the months and years after the accident was as toxic as the air around Chernobyl, and those in Ukraine with an axe to grind were only too happy to use the accident to their ends. Nationalists, not just in Ukraine but in Belarus as well, took up the environmental cause.

This coincided with the ongoing *glasnost* and *perestroika* programmes being put in place by Mikhail Gorbachev. Having ridden out his first year in power and made it through the Chernobyl disaster, Gorbachev had gradually asserted his control over the Politburo and was implementing his plans to reform the Soviet Union in earnest. It was for him an ideological imperative, a crusade – designed to restructure the Union, particularly the economy, and prevent it dwindling into international insignificance. He was unable or unwilling to see where these new policies might lead, however. Chernobyl had helped whip up nationalist and anti-authoritarian feelings in some of the Soviet Union's component states and in satellite nations such as East Germany and Poland. In this situation, an old-style Soviet leader would have paused any liberalization programmes (if they'd allowed them in the first place) and ordered a crackdown. Gorbachev, however, pressed on. In June 1988 he persuaded the Nineteenth All-Union Conference of the Communist Party to wave through his proposals for opening up the political process and allowing the Soviet Union's most free and participatory elections to date the following year.

Naturally, those who most enthusiastically took this as their call to action were not the mass of the Soviet people, rushing to the polls to support their leader, but the groups who favoured change, more liberalization, greater democracy and, most alarmingly, independence. Five months after the conference, environmental activists in Kyiv, calling themselves *Zelenyi Svit* (Green World), tested the waters by holding the first mass rally in Ukraine not organized by the Communist Party. This was significant. In April the previous year, on the first anniversary of Chernobyl, the authorities in Kyiv had successfully stopped a rally commemorating the accident by a combination of KGB harassment of the event organizers and by closing off and even digging up roads around the planned demonstration route. Now, less than a year later, Communist Party officials in Kyiv were allowing 10,000 protesters to gather together and openly criticize the regime's environmental record.

Two hours into the rally came an event that would have far-reaching consequences. Physicist Ivan Makar took to the stage and told the crowd before him that they needed to fight for economic and political sovereignty for Ukraine – in effect, independence. The KGB switched off Makar's microphone but he carried on speaking and the crowd began to chant the word 'Mi-cro-phone' in unison, urging the secret police to let the speaker be heard. 'Mi-cro-phone' would be become one of the slogans of the burgeoning anti-Moscow movement in Ukraine and would also be used as the title of a documentary about the environmental effects of Chernobyl. From this moment, the environmental, democratic and nationalist movements in Ukraine, and in other parts of the Soviet Union, began to coalesce into ever-more organized opposition to their Communist Party controllers. This was precisely the opposite of what Mikhail Gorbachev had intended when he introduced *glasnost*. In his mind the policy would mobilize activists and intellectuals who supported his reforms against inept, corrupt or complacent Party officials and help make the Soviet Union the socialist wonderland it was destined to be. But the groups that *glasnost* gave voice to were, in the main, not on Gorbachev's side. To them he was part of the problem, not the solution. In the meantime, by marginalizing the hardliners in the Politburo and in the Communist Party, Gorbachev had left himself isolated on that front as well.

By the start of 1989 it was clear that Gorbachev was no longer leading events in the Soviet Union and was struggling to keep up with the rapidly changing political landscape. To appease potential supporters in Ukraine, he had supported the formation of a group known as the Movement for Perestroika, more commonly known as Rukh, against the wishes of the powerful, conservative Kyiv Party boss Volodymyr Shcherbytsky. Yet all this did was to earn Gorbachev even greater enmity from Shcherbytsky, whom he had already antagonized in 1986 over the controversial May Day parade, and make him beholden to Rukh, which immediately called for a programme of economic and political liberalization far beyond anything the Soviet leader desired. From an environmental point of view, Rukh also demanded that all RBMK-powered Ukrainian nuclear power stations, including Chernobyl, be shut down.

Rukh was able to put its proposals before the people in the national elections of March–April 1989, which Gorbachev had promised at the Nineteenth Communist Party Conference the previous June. Under Gorbachev's new voting proposals, the Soviet Congress of People's Deputies was expanded to 2,250 representatives, two-thirds of whom would be elected directly by the people. In the previous Soviet elections, in 1984, all 1,500 deputies had been appointed by the Communist Party.

In this first test of people power during Gorbachev's rule, Chernobyl-inspired environmental issues played a major role. The Rukh party in Ukraine made ecological safety a key part of its platform, as did the Sajidus Party in Lithuania, where the Ignalina Nuclear Power Plant had become a symbol of both the dangers posed by RBMK reactors and the nuclear imperialism imposed by Moscow on the rest of the Soviet Union. The self-styled Independent candidates from parties such as Rukh and Sajidus faced an uphill battle to get themselves elected in the face of a mostly politically unengaged populace and an immensely powerful Communist Party machine that controlled the levers of power and influence.

When the new Soviet Congress convened after the election, the vast majority of its deputies – 1,958 – had been endorsed by or were affiliated to the Communist Party; just 292 were Independents. Nevertheless, this was an impressive achievement. The Independents would go on to form a powerful bloc in the new Congress, forcefully pushing their anti-nuclear power, environmentalist and nationalist agenda. Their ranks would include future post-Soviet luminaries such as Alla Yaroshinskaya, the journalist who would become one of President Boris Yeltsin's advisors, and Yuriy Shcherbak, the writer, diplomat and founder of the Party of Greens of Ukraine. Their very presence in the parliament was significant in itself, and it helped to legitimize popular protests within the Soviet Union. In Belarus, which had been subjected to even more nuclear contamination than Ukraine after Chernobyl, the authorities were powerless to stop an anti-nuclear power mass meeting in the capital Minsk on 30 September. This gathering of 30,000 people would have been unthinkable just months before.

By then, however, everything had changed. In June 1989 Solidarity had won a huge majority in Communist Poland's first free elections, followed by Soviet-supporting Hungary dismantling its physical border with Austria later that same month. One by one, Communist regimes across Eastern Europe were swept away, mostly peacefully. The most symbolic moment happened on 9 November when East German border guards

Protest against the Ignalina power plant in Lithuania, 1988.

stood aside as protesters in the eastern part of the city scaled the Berlin Wall and began to tear it down. A year earlier, in response to the first strikes, demonstrations and protests against one-party rule, Mikhail Gorbachev had publicly stated that he would take no action to help any of the regimes under threat from their dissident populations. It is possible that he believed *perestroika* and *glasnost* would at last save the day, but liberal protest movements within the Soviet Union were growing and Gorbachev's conservative enemies were beginning to mobilize against him.

The following year, the Soviet Union itself began to unravel. On 11 March 1990 Lithuania became the first of the Soviet republics to declare independence. It is no coincidence that Lithuania had been one of the areas where the post-Chernobyl, anti-nuclear, environmental protests had been strongest. Ironically, following the crippling economic and political blockade that Mikhail Gorbachev imposed on the errant republic, independent Lithuania's new environmentally friendly rulers were forced not just to reconsider plans to close the country's controversial RBMK-powered Ignalina nuclear power station but to begin building new nuclear reactors too.

But nuclear power remained a key factor in the rest of the Soviet Union after Lithuania's departure, not least in Ukraine. In federal elections there in 1990, Chernobyl remained a central issue and the anti-nuclear Rukh party and its allies won around a quarter of the seats in the Ukrainian assembly. At rallies, campaigners carried placards denouncing the Communist Party and attacking the mainly Russian and Russian-speaking personnel running Ukraine's nuclear power plants. Day by day the anti-nuclear and nationalist agendas were merging into one

– especially as one of the outcomes of Ukraine's 1990 elections saw the country's government agree to a five-year moratorium on building new nuclear power plants. In another concession, the new Ukrainian parliament approved a special commission to look into how Moscow and Kyiv authorities had handled the Chernobyl disaster, and how much information they had withheld and tried to cover up. By October 1990 the Rukh party announced that its environmental aims had largely been fulfilled and that its new priority was the achievement of independence for Ukraine from the Soviet Union.

Following the revolutions of 1989, Lithuania's declaration of independence and now the Rukh party's statement of intent, the hard men in the Kremlin decided that enough was enough. On 19 August 1991 a group of conspirators led by KGB chief Vladimir Kryuchkov, defence minister Dimitry Yazov and vice-president Gennady Yanayev launched a coup d'état against Mikhail Gorbachev in which they intended to roll back democratic reforms and reinstate one-party rule. The attempted seizure of power failed and all of its instigators were arrested, but Gorbachev had lost all authority by the end of the three-day crisis. The president of Russia, Boris Yeltsin, emerged as the hero in putting down the coup and, seeing that the Soviet Union's days were numbered, he made it known he was not opposed to the constituent states of the Union going their own way.

On 24 August 1991 Mikhail Gorbachev resigned as the General Secretary of the Communist Party of the Soviet Union and, that same day, Ukraine's Supreme Council issued a declaration of independence. Belarus followed suit the next day. By 8 December a looser, informal alliance called the Commonwealth of Independent States (CIS) had been established: this involved .

nine countries, including Russia and Belarus, as well as Ukraine, which did ratify the agreement but did not subsequently ratify the Charter that would make it a member. On 25 December Mikhail Gorbachev bowed to the inevitable and resigned as president. The Soviet Union was officially dissolved and the rest of its constituent states became independent.

Seventy years of Soviet history had come to an abrupt end, but life went on. Politically, economically and socially, the entire region was in turmoil and would remain so for several years. Of the many thousands of issues that needed to be addressed in the post-Soviet era, one pressing problem was what to do about Chernobyl. Now operated by an independent Ukraine, the plant was still operational, but questions remained about whether it should be and what to do about the ongoing containment operation on the Unit 4 reactor.

Chapter 7:

AFTERMATH

It's reasonable to expect the explosion at Chernobyl to have signalled the end of its existence as a working facility. Yet, somehow, it would be another 14 years before the plant was finally closed for good, having outlasted the Soviet Union that built it by almost a decade. How that happened is a story of politics, power, international intrigue, ecological anxiety and engineering innovation.

After the accident, Chernobyl's Unit 4 reactor was little more than a molten mass of metal, concrete, graphite and uranium; a smouldering bomb site that was one of the most toxic places on earth. But, just metres away, the Unit 1, 2 and 3 reactors were still fully operational – and, in cold, hard, practical terms, it made little sense to keep them switched off once the fire at the Unit 4 reactor had been put out and the worst of its radioactive

A shift supervisor working at Chernobyl's Unit 3 reactor in 2010, helping with the decommissioning process.

emissions contained. One by one the reactors were restarted and reconnected to Ukraine's national grid. Experts and government officials went out of their way to pretend that this was all perfectly normal, but the reality on the ground was quite different. The whole Chernobyl site was still affected by radiation, with some areas worse than others. Engineers and operators at the plant had to be regularly rotated from reactor to reactor, so that no employee spent too long working at Unit 3, next door to the ruined Unit 4 reactor site.

The reason the world's most notorious power station kept going until December 2000 was simple: Chernobyl generated 6 per cent of Ukraine's electricity, and the country simply could not do without the energy it supplied. The West in particular was not happy about this. The United States, United Kingdom

and other European nations insisted that Chernobyl was not safe and that it had to close. From the moment of independence, and for almost the next 10 years, Ukraine's governments were able to use the West's misgivings about Chernobyl to their own political and economic ends.

The Soviet Union was weak in the years leading up to its fall, but after its dissolution the independent states that had once comprised it were even weaker. Those that got back on their feet soonest would be best placed to recover once the dust from its collapse had settled. Russia was sure to bounce back quickest, but, in theory, Ukraine should not have been too far behind. It was the former Soviet Union's second most populous nation with the second largest economy. Yet these two factors also made Ukraine vulnerable. Whereas before it had been Russia's comrade-in-arms within the Soviet Union, now it was a potential rival. On the day it achieved independence, 24 August 1991, Ukraine suddenly found itself in possession of 1,800 atomic warheads, making it the world's third largest nuclear power behind the United States and Russia. In which direction those missiles would point – west, towards Europe and the USA, or north, towards Russia – was a global issue of crucial importance.

Unwilling to bear the cost and responsibility of managing this arsenal, Ukraine, along with Belarus and Kazakhstan, which had also inherited Soviet nuclear missiles, announced they were willing to give up those weapons if they received certain security assurances. In December 1994 the three nations signed the Budapest Memorandum alongside Russia, the United Kingdom and the United States. By its terms, Ukraine, Belarus and Kazakhstan gave up their nuclear weapons; and in return the other three signatories promised to respect each country's territorial integrity.

As far as Ukraine's president Leonid Kravchuk was concerned, this now meant that his country was safe: Russia was appeased by Ukraine's nuclear 'surrender', and by disarming itself Ukraine was to obtain hundreds of millions of much-needed dollars in aid. But in reality, the Budapest Memorandum weakened Ukraine and made its post-Soviet recovery that much more difficult. The memorandum stated that none of the other signatories would attack Ukraine, but crucially it did not oblige any of them to come to Ukraine's military assistance if one or more of the other signatories broke the agreement. This is one of the reasons why neither the United Kingdom nor the United States acted when Russian-backed forces invaded Sevastopol on Ukraine's Black Sea coast in 2014.

Hemmed in between a Russia bent on asserting itself as a world power and a West eager to capitalize on the gains made from the end of the Cold War, Ukraine's leaders knew that, if they showed any further signs of vulnerability, their country could be swallowed up in the new regional map that was being redrawn across Europe. East Germany was gone, Czechoslovakia had been split in two and the Balkans were in turmoil. Who was to say that Ukraine could not be partitioned or absorbed at some point into a Greater Russia? The country had to be kept viable, and the means of doing this lay in protecting the energy sources that powered its businesses and its industry, and to make sure the lights stayed on in people's homes – in short, to keep the generators running. Above all, and despite the promises and campaigning to close down Ukraine's nuclear power stations in the run-up to independence, it meant that all of them, including Chernobyl, had to be kept going. There was even a provision for this in the Budapest Memorandum, which obliged Russia to continue supplying Ukraine's nuclear power stations with the Russian-made enriched uranium on which the former Soviet state's reactors ran.

At the same time, the United States and other Western nations eased the pressure they had been applying on Leonid Kravchuk to decommission Chernobyl as quickly as possible. This was because Ukraine's president told them the only way he could close the plant was if the G7 group of countries made up the economic shortfall this would cause by supplying Ukraine with even more aid from their own coffers. In 1993 the G7 had set up the Nuclear Safety Account with the European Bank for Reconstruction and Development (EBRD), to which each of its member nations contributed funds, and from which each of the old Eastern Bloc's nations could withdraw money if any of their RBMK-powered nuclear reactors needed upgrading or repair. It was not intended to provide limitless free funds to Ukraine,

Lithuania, Kazakhstan and the other former Soviet states whose nuclear sites were most in need of attention; it was created more as a failsafe in the event of another major nuclear power accident. It is ironic, then, that in order to protect funds accumulated to prevent another Chernobyl-style catastrophe, Chernobyl itself was allowed to remain open. The West did not give up, however, and it periodically put pressure on Ukraine to shut down the plant. In early 1995, for example, the G7 threatened to withhold $85 million in Ukrainian aid payments unless the country put together a timetable for Chernobyl's closure. Leonid Kuchma, Ukraine's new president, managed to string along the West for a while until the ultimatum was withdrawn and then kept the plant running as normal.

Finally, a compromise was reached at the end of 1995, when the G7 and the EU reached an agreement with Ukraine that it would completely decommission Chernobyl by 2000 in return for an aid package of $2.3 billion to pay for the plant's closure and the construction of two new nuclear reactors at Khmelnytskyi and Rivne in western Ukraine, as well as the refurbishment of several coal-fired plants across the country. Almost a decade after Chernobyl's Unit 4 reactor exploded, a definitive plan for the plant's demise was finally put in place.

The possibility of keeping Chernobyl open at all had been made possible by makeshift remedial works carried out in the weeks and months after the accident. When the Shcherbina Commission was established the day after the disaster to both contain and investigate the catastrophe at Chernobyl, one of its earliest recommendations was that a protective casing be built around the destroyed Unit 4 reactor as soon as possible. Mikhail

Gorbachev ordered the Ministry of Medium Machine Building boss Efim Slavsky to carry out this task, effectively telling the 87-year-old engineer that his department had constructed Chernobyl and developed the faulty RBMK reactor, so it was his job to fix the problem.

Eight weeks after the explosion, Efim Slavsky gave the go-ahead for work on what became known as the sarcophagus to begin. He put together a team of architects, physicists and builders from the MMMB to create a casing for the ruined Unit 4 reactor that would contain its radioactive emissions and allow the rest of the Chernobyl site to remain in use. The presence of MMMB men at Chernobyl created a degree of tension at the power plant, which was operated by the rival Ministry of Energy. There was no love lost between the two government departments and cooperation between them on the sarcophagus project was virtually non-existent. In effect, the MMMB had to build the Sarcophagus in enemy territory.

Designers submitted a number of plans for Slavsky to consider. One involved excavating a cavern under the reactor into which it would fall and in time be swallowed by the earth; another proposed filling what was left of the Unit 4 reactor hall with hollow lead balls, or, in another approach, crushed boulders. Slavsky himself was tempted simply to pour thousands of tonnes of concrete over the whole ruin and hope for the best. This, like most of the other suggestions, was impractical. Whatever the reactor was finally encased in needed some sort of organized structure and include provision for access, so that the accident site could be maintained and properly ventilated.

Finally, a solution of sorts was reached, and Gorbachev told Slavsky to complete it by September 1986, just four months after work on the sarcophagus began. With little time to lose and a lack of expertise and experience – nothing like the Chernobyl explosion had ever happened before, after all – Slavsky's team improvised a plan to erect what was essentially the world's largest flat-packed bunker over the remains of the Unit 4 reactor building. Radioactive dust was recognized as a problem before building work could begin: easily kicked up by people and vehicles moving in and around the site, with the potential to create a sandstorm if any helicopters were used. This issue was solved by dousing the building area in pulped beetroot, which was found to be suitably absorbent without being too sticky.

Because radiation levels were so high inside the reactor – up to 10,000 röntgens per hour, 20 times a lethal dose – slabs of reinforced concrete for the sarcophagus walls were formed off-site and assembled in a modular fashion before being moved to the building area around the Unit 4 reactor. Remotely controlled vehicles and armoured cars brought material as close to the reactor as possible, with the final fix carried out by men working in five-minute bursts of activity. Thousands of tonnes of concrete were poured to make the Sarcophagus's walls and ceiling, with work carried out 24 hours a day. Two massive, heavy-duty cranes, imported at huge cost from Germany, manoeuvred a series of steel frames around the reactor, each one filled with rubble against which the sarcophagus's walls could be erected. One side of the structure was constructed as a series of four giant steps in order to cover piles of radioactive debris that had accumulated where the reactor hall roof and one of the walls had collapsed. This part of the sarcophagus was known as the Cascade Wall and was 50m (164ft) long and 12m (39ft) high.

As the sarcophagus neared completion, there was one final

job. What remained of the reactor hall roof was still covered in tonnes of radioactive graphite, strewn around in thousands of lumps that had to be cleared away. Initially, engineers used remotely controlled vehicles to carry out this dangerous task, but the devices kept burning out, breaking down or falling over as they picked their way through the rubble. Finally, it was decided that the operation had to be carried out by hand.

This is when General Nikolai Tarakanov's army of 3,000 'biorobots' took to the reactor hall roof (*see* Chapter 3). Grabbing the graphite piece by piece, the young army recruits threw each block down into the open Sarcophagus so that it could be entombed inside what was becoming a vast nuclear dustbin. It took 12 days to remove all the graphite, but once this was complete the final phase could take place – putting the sarcophagus's cover in place. This was no easy task, as the building was 70m long (230ft) long. After much head scratching, a plan was devised: a lead cabin capable of holding four people was dangled over the opening of the sarcophagus from one of the two German cranes, acting as a command centre as the other crane lowered a 70m (230ft) steel beam nicknamed 'the Mammoth' into place horizontally along the open roof of the sarcophagus. At huge personal risk, 60 volunteers swarmed over the frame of the sarcophagus while this happened, fixing panels that extended across from the Mammoth to the structure's walls on either side to form a solid, flat roof. Tonnes of concrete were then poured over the panels, across which were stretched fishing-trawler nets, intended to give the concrete extra strength and rigidity as it dried.

By early November, two months later than scheduled, the main structure was ready. Engineers then installed a ventilation system, to stop the still-active core inside from overheating. A sprinkler system was also added, in the vain hope that it would put out any fires if a chain reaction inside the reactor spontaneously happened: there was still 180 tonnes of nuclear fuel somewhere in the reactor, but no one knew where it was; in the right – or wrong – circumstances, it could overheat, initiate fission and explode.

The finished Sarcophagus was never going to win any design awards. Architecturally, it was the most brutal of all the Soviet Union's brutalist edifices. It was one of the largest, too, comprising almost 8,000 tonnes of steel and more than 1 million m^3 (3.5 million ft^3) of concrete and crushed stone. Crudely constructed, it was ugly and ungainly, while its radioactivity-suppressing qualities were questionable, but it was better than nothing. It was probably more effective as a visual symbol than anything else, a sign that action had been taken and that the site was safer that it had been. It was clear, however, that the sarcophagus was never going to be a long-term solution, even though it had cost an estimated $5 billion to build. In the meantime, Chernobyl's workforce had to keep putting themselves in harm's way so that the plant could keep running.

One week after the sarcophagus was finished, Efim Slavsky was summoned to the office of Soviet prime minister Nikolai Ryzhkov, thanked for his many years of service and ordered to resign.

For those left behind to work at Chernobyl, life, surprisingly, was not all bad. There was the radiation to deal with, of course, but workers were assured that the Sarcophagus had taken care of that. Protocols were also put in place so that staff did not spend too much time in close proximity to the Sarcophagus, or indeed at the Unit 3 reactor next door. In addition, around $400 million was spent on the remaining reactors over the next few years, improving their safety and performance.

Did these measures reassure most of the 6,000 employees who worked on the site until its final closure? Or were they believing what they wanted to believe? Jobs in the region during the last years of the Soviet Union and the early, chaotic days of an independent Ukraine were hard to come by, and those on offer at Chernobyl were more secure and better paid than most.

The majority of Chernobyl's post-accident workforce also got to live in Slavutych, the new city built to replace the now-abandoned Pripyat. Like in Pripyat, the apartments in Slavutych were larger and more comfortable than was the norm in the Soviet Union, its shops better-stocked and its public services better-resourced (*see* Chapter 5). Labouring day after day at the world's most notorious accident site was a price many people were prepared to pay in return for the lifestyle it offered. There was dismay at the plant whenever the international community reminded Ukraine's government of its commitment to wind down the facility – and rejoicing each time the politicians in Kyiv reneged on this agreement once they had secured the aid they needed from the West.

Signs that the 1986 disaster was not the end of Chernobyl's troubles came in October 1991, when a fire broke out in the Unit 2 reactor's turbine hall, destroying part of the roof. Although this accident was nowhere near the scale of what had happened five years earlier, it was not an incident that could be hushed up. Reluctantly, but sensibly, Kyiv's parliament voted to permanently close down the reactor with immediate effect. But just two years later those same politicians overturned this decision. At the same time, they cancelled plans to close the two other remaining reactors, Units 1 and 3, by 1995. Now, they declared, all three reactors would stay running until they reached the end of their operating lives. This ultimately did not happen – international pressure saw to that – but it was proof that Chernobyl remained a troubled and troubling place. Reviled in the years before the end of the Soviet Union, it was held up as an icon of Ukraine's nationhood afterwards.

Things took an even more bizarre turn in 1997, at a ceremony at the plant to mark Chernobyl's 20th anniversary. One of the guests of honour that day was none other than Viktor Bryukhanov. He had left the site in disgrace 11 years earlier, but was now treated to a standing ovation when he came to the podium to speak. So important had Chernobyl become to Ukraine's idea of itself as a nation now free of Soviet (i.e. Russian) control that it was almost as though the accident had never happened.

But it had, as organizations such as the G7, the EU, the World Bank and the EBRD never tired of telling Ukraine's leaders. Finally, succumbing to international compulsion, and with the deadline looming for a $2.3 billion aid package that was conditional on Chernobyl's decommissioning, Ukraine's government closed the plant for good on 15 December 2000. By this time, only the Unit 3 reactor was still running, the Unit 1 reactor having been shut down in 1996, yet it was nevertheless a landmark moment. Environmentalists and anti-nuclear power campaigners worldwide celebrated. Others, though, were less happy. The day before the power station ceased operating, it was visited by Ukraine's president, Leonid Kuchma, accompanied by the prime ministers of Russia and Belarus, along with the US energy secretary Bill Richardson. As they toured the site, the political dignitaries were greeted by workers wearing black armbands in protest against the closure. Few could have imagined such a display of loyalty from employees on the morning on 27 April 1986, when the site's Unit 4 reactor was blazing out of control, churning tonnes of radioactive material into the atmosphere, and plant operatives and firefighters lay dying painfully in Pripyat and Kyiv hospitals.

Once Chernobyl's fate had been resolved, technicians were free to carry on with an enterprise that had been in the works since 1992: the building of a new sarcophagus for the Unit 4 reactor.

It had been only a matter of months before Efim Slavsky's 1986 sarcophagus had begun to crack and leak radiation. Six years later, Ukraine's government established an international competition to design a new cover for the reactor. In the spirit of international cooperation, the G7 pledged $300 million toward the estimated build cost of $760 million, establishing a Chernobyl Shelter Fund with the EBRD. The plan at first was to have the new sarcophagus built by 2005, five years after Chernobyl's final closure. But it was not until 2007 that the winning contractor for the shelter was announced, a French consortium called Novarka. Its intention was to cover the existing sarcophagus and a wide area of land around it inside a giant, hermetically sealed, sliding steel arch.

At 165m long (540ft) and 110m high (360ft), and with a span of 257m (843ft), the finished structure is larger than London's Wembley Stadium or the Superdome in New Orleans, and is taller than the Statue of Liberty. It weighs 36,000 tonnes. Work began in 2010 and was originally due to be completed in 2012, but the inevitable delays associated with such a vast and dangerous civil engineering project meant this was pushed back to 2013, and then 2015. Ultimately, the new Sarcophagus would not be fully completed until 2019. It was not actually built in situ over the old sarcophagus but was put together 300m (984ft) away. The panels making up the building were manufactured in Italy, then shipped to Ukraine and transported by truck to the site. When the main body of the edifice was assembled, the whole construction was moved on rails into position over the old sarcophagus. Once in place, the end walls were fitted. Officially known as the New Safe Confinement (NSC) structure, it is the biggest moveable land-based construction ever built. It is planned to remain in use for 100 years. The final cost was around double the original estimate, the vast majority paid for by overseas governments.

Inside the new sarcophagus, the old sarcophagus sits at its centre like a museum exhibit or a ruined ancient temple. Piece by piece the old Sarcophagus is being dismantled by remotely controlled robotic devices and cranes, allowing technicians to explore the remains of the Unit 4 reactor and remove nuclear fuel and toxic waste material. If all goes to plan, the new sarcophagus will eventually be nothing more than an empty hangar.

Meanwhile, the rest of the site – reactor Units 1, 2 and 3, the turbine halls, the control rooms, administration buildings, machinery, fuel, waste products and even contaminated soil and water – is being safely decontaminated and dismantled. It is a painstaking and slow process. The three remaining reactor Units will not be demolished and cleared away to storage sites until 2064, 78 years after the accident. The hundreds of tonnes of used nuclear fuel from the power station are being stored in specially constructed tanks at the ISF-2 facility opened in April 2021 at the Chernobyl site. It is the largest spent-nuclear

The New Safe Confinement structure in 2021.

fuel storage facility in the world, and its operators maintain any material kept there will remain safe for at least 100 years. The bulk of the items currently kept in ISF-2's tanks are the 21,217 used fuel rods from Chernobyl's reactors, accumulated over its years of operation – graphite-tipped, boron-filled rods just like those that helped to initiate the Unit 4 reactor disaster. Less contaminated waste from Chernobyl is being treated, 'washed' and reprocessed so that it can be made safe, then compacted into solid blocks and buried at the Vektor disposal site 17km (10.5 miles) from Chernobyl.

No one involved in the repurposing of Chernobyl pretends it will be a quick or easy process. The cleansing of the site – if it can ever fully be cleansed – will be measured in decades at best. But Ukraine and international governments and scientific and aid agencies have worked together – not always easily – to devise what appear so far to be workable solutions to the many issues that need to be tackled at Chernobyl. In the meantime, since its closure, the plant has enjoyed an afterlife as a visitor attraction. Intrepid tourists have been able to explore the site's control rooms, walk down the 'golden corridor' and look at the turbine halls – under carefully supervised conditions – since 2011. In 2019 visitor numbers leapt by more than 30 per cent following the release of the critically acclaimed HBO television drama *Chernobyl*. Many former Chernobyl staff now act as tour guides.

Understandably, most of the financial, scientific, political and practical activity following the Chernobyl disaster has been based at the power station itself. But away from the former nuclear facility interesting things are happening inside the vast area of land evacuated in the aftermath of the accident.

He didn't know it at the time, and it was certainly not his intention, but when the Soviet prime minister Nikolai Ryzhkov approved the 30km (19 mile) exclusion zone around Chernobyl on 2 May 1986, just days after the disaster, he was initiating what would become one of the most important ecological experiments of modern times.

In its heyday, just before the Unit 4 reactor blast, Pripyat was one of the Soviet Union's newest, best-resourced and well-organized cities. Its population of 50,000 was mostly young and well-educated, the majority employed at Chernobyl 3km (1.8 miles) away. Thirty-six hours after the accident, all of that had changed. Those 50,000 men, women and children had gone forever, relocated in record time to safe sites in Kyiv and other cities, towns and villages in western Ukraine. Pripyat became a ghost town, its buildings abandoned at the shortest of notice, with beds unmade and breakfast things not yet cleared away. In just a matter of weeks, weeds began to poke through cracks in the city's paving stones and tarmac roads; within a month or two the warm spring weather ensured that Pripyat's well-kept parks and orderly grass verges were transforming into wild meadows.

The city now exists in a condition of 'arrested decay' – a concept inspired by the former gold-mining settlement of Bodie, California. This was a boom town in the 1870s and '80s. When the gold ran out so did most of the population, and the place was virtually deserted by the late 1890s. The buildings remained, however, many of them still furnished and filled with the former inhabitants' possessions, and in the 1960s California's state government took possession of the existing ruins and decided to preserve what was left of Bodie in arrested decay. This means that they are allowing nature to reclaim the town and leaving its structures to decline, with only minimal human interference to prevent their complete collapse – Bodie is, after all, a popular tourist attraction, and endangering its visitors' lives is bad for business.

The authorities took a similar approach to Pripyat, and for similar reasons. Time has progressed and radiation levels have declined, and in 2011 Pripyat was officially designated a tourist attraction. Radioactivity there is lower than it once was but it remains higher than recommended, especially in the city's several hotspots. Tourists are advised not to linger too long as they wander Pripyat's overgrown streets and peer through the windows of its shops and public buildings, each room a snapshot of a vanished era. The telltale bleep of the radiation monitor each visitor is obliged to wear acts as a warning sign that things are getting too hot and it's time to move on. For safety reasons, it is not possible to enter most of Pripyat's buildings because they are in dangerous states of disrepair, either from decay, vandalism or theft. Over the years, unauthorized armies of scavengers raided the city, stealing as much metal, scrap and sellable goods as they could find; you will search in vain today for an intact iron handrail on a Pripyat staircase or a metal window frame. Standing water from rainfall has seeped through building roofs into apartments, so that blown plaster has fallen off the walls in clumps and scabs of peeling paint infect the walls like some disfiguring skin disease.

As well as authorized tourists, Pripyat is also a magnet for a guerrilla army of unofficial visitors. Known as stalkers, they are thrill-seeking adrenaline junkies such as base-jumpers, free-runners and wild campers. Most stalkers are young Ukrainian men who sneak into the exclusion zone to spend time exploring the city and the surrounding countryside on their own terms and at their own risk. They sleep overnight in abandoned buildings, drink water from rivers and streams, and eat fruit plucked from the thousands of trees that have grown in the area since the disaster. Because the exclusion zone has been devoid of major human interference for so long, the local water supply is remarkably uncontaminated and the wild fruit and vegetables are pesticide free and therefore organic. The area is still radioactive, of course, but the attraction of stalking lies in knowing or finding out where the safest sites are and reducing the risk of exposure. Anyone caught stalking risks imprisonment, but in reality the security guards patrolling Chernobyl's exclusion zone usually turn a blind eye to any incursions.

For the stalkers, the exclusion zone is a giant adventure playground. In fact, it even has its own fun fair – although the amusement park in Pripyat has been closed for business for more than 35 years. Today, its rusting, creaking Ferris wheel has become a symbol of the irreversible decay that is slowly taking over the city. Pripyat's buildings are becoming increasingly difficult to even see, hidden behind countless stands of trees whose tops are now higher than the city's tallest tower blocks. Before long Pripyat will become a modern-day Angkor Wat, an abandoned civilization lost to the forest and awaiting rediscovery.

But Pripyat is not completely devoid of life. Eagles roost on building tops and wild horses, released into the exclusion zone 10 years after the accident, roam freely in and out of the city. Descended from the household pets that teams of liquidators sought to destroy in the first weeks after the disaster, dogs and cats are everywhere in Pripyat and the countryside nearby. At constant risk of predation by wolves, starvation, contamination,

The Ferris wheel in the Pripyat amusement park.

disease and other threats, their lifespans are short, averaging around five years. In recent years, animal rescue organizations including SPCA International and the Clean Futures Fund have set up vaccination and sterilization programmes for the exclusion zone's wild dog and cat populations, sending in specially trained and equipped vets to administer medication and perform operations. Many of the security guards working in the exclusion zone have unofficially adopted wild dogs and cats, too,

bringing them food or building safe shelters for them against the elements and larger predators. Other animals that have weathered the nuclear storm and which today thrive in the human-free environment of Chernobyl's exclusion zone include deer, lynx, beaver, bears, wild boar and elk. Radioactivity remains a problem and some animals, when tested, are found to have heightened levels of caesium-137 in their bodies. This is usually because of the food they eat – wild mushrooms in particular known for their ability to absorb radioactive isotopes from the soil many years after exposure. But, in general, scientific studies show that the net environmental effect of the Chernobyl disaster has been *more* species and greater biodiversity within the exclusion zone than before the accident. This increase is almost exclusively because of the absence of human activity. Even in the face of the worst nuclear disaster of all time, people remain the most toxic influence on the natural world.

Perhaps it's a mixed blessing, then, that after decades of splendid isolation Chernobyl's exclusion zone is slowly becoming home to human inhabitants again. More than 300,000 people were relocated from the worst affected areas of Ukraine and Belarus in the days after the explosion, and the exclusion zone that was set up thereafter remained almost completely empty of residents for more than 20 years. In 2010 the government of Belarus announced that it would allow the resettlement of large areas of its portion of the exclusion zone, and 211 villages and hamlets previously designated as unsafe were reclassified and approved for human habitation. Financial aid and industrial start-up programmes were offered in the country's Gomel and Mogilev regions, close to the border with Ukraine, from which more than 137,000 Belarusians had been displaced. These are important agricultural and forestry areas for Belarus and their loss for more than 25 years had been a drain on the country's economy. More than 1,300km (800 miles) of new roads have been laid, thousands of houses built and the local infrastructure upgraded at a cost of $2.2 billion. In marginal areas, where radiation levels hover between acceptable and not acceptable, 498 villages and settlements are being carefully monitored.

Land studies have also been carried out to assess radiation levels across the exclusion zone. Areas where caesium-137 and strontium-90 deposits are found have been assessed and those with low amounts have been approved for agricultural use, while zones with higher levels will be reforested instead. Ukraine is taking a more cautious approach and its part of the exclusion zone remains largely uninhabited. A few, mostly elderly, residents refused to leave when the mass evacuation of 1986 was carried out and the authorities in the end allowed them to stay. Since then, a scattering of mainly rural folk have drifted back to their old farmsteads and smallholdings, claiming they were unable to adjust to life in the new villages, towns and cities they were sent to. These returnees have not been removed and, in most cases, have shown no ill effects, increased incidences of cancers or any of the other adverse conditions associated with overexposure to radiation.

This is not to paint too rosy a picture of the aftermath of Chernobyl. Its effects continue to be felt, not just within the exclusion zone but much further afield. Estimates of the accident's long-term death toll vary widely – from 4,000, according to the United Nations, to 90,000, as proposed by Greenpeace. Whatever the number, it is too high. In addition, there are the cancers and other radiation-related illnesses to take into account. The World Health Organization estimates the accident is responsible for up to 5,000 instances of thyroid cancer in children who were aged 0–18 at the time of the explosion. There has also been a concerning rise in a condition known as microsatellite instability (MSI) across those parts of Ukraine, Belarus and Russia that lay under the flight path of the nuclear cloud produced by the Unit 4 reactor explosion. MSI is a condition that prevents DNA from replicating and repairing itself, and it has been detected in increased numbers among the children of Soviet firefighters, soldiers and workers who were involved in either the explosion or the containment process at Chernobyl. Beyond the medical toll, Chernobyl has decimated the economies of Ukraine, Belarus and, to a lesser extent Russia, for years to come.

The Chernobyl disaster demonstrated just how in thrall Ukraine was to Russia, and this has been a source of resentment and tension ever since. It was Russia that oversaw the plant from Moscow, Russia that supplied its fuel, Russia that took over the investigation once the accident happened, and Russia that blamed Ukrainian operatives when it disclosed the disaster's causes. If nothing else, Chernobyl made Ukraine's leaders vow never to be so dependent on their northern neighbour again. For years after the accident Russia continued to provide Ukraine's nuclear reactors with the fuel they needed – meaning it could threaten to withhold that fuel, too, if it wanted to put pressure on Ukraine. The 2014 invasion of Sevastopol by Russian-backed troops was a case in point. There are many reasons why Ukraine surrendered the Black Sea port and a large area of land around it without too much of a fight – the presence of many pro-Russian officers and troops within the Ukrainian army defending Sevastopol, for example – but the loss of the strategically important city that acts as the base for Russia's Black Sea Fleet at least allowed the government in Kyiv to avoid an escalation of the conflict with Moscow. Ambassadors were summoned and strongly worded diplomatic notes of displeasure were issued, but Ukraine's ultimate acceptance of Russia's annexation of part of its territory can in part be ascribed to the former's dependency on the latter to fulfil its energy needs.

Chernobyl may have long been closed by then, but Ukraine's 15 remaining nuclear reactors, which generated 50 per cent of the country's electricity, were hungry for Russian-supplied fuel.

Ukraine has steadily been decreasing its reliance on Russian uranium ever since. In 2016, Ukraine began building a nuclear power station that will use spent fuel. In atomic energy generation terms, this is as close to recycling as the industry gets, employing retreated fuel that has already been used in an existing nuclear reactor. This shift in supplier did not meet with Russia's approval, which was certainly one of Ukraine's intentions. Moscow retaliated by attacking Westinghouse's credibility, making unsubstantiated claims that the company's nuclear fuel was unsafe. In September 2021 the government in Kyiv announced that it had signed an agreement for Westinghouse to build four new nuclear reactors in Ukraine. In December 2021 Russia began massing tens of thousands of armed soldiers along its border with Ukraine. The timing is not coincidental. Peace talks between Russia and Ukraine over the ownership of Crimea had recently broken down, and incidents such as the Westinghouse deal were proof to Russia's president, Vladimir Putin, that Ukraine was turning too far to the West and could perhaps, in what was his nightmare scenario, be on the road to joining NATO.

This was one of the reasons why Putin's armed forces invaded Ukraine in February 2022. One of the first sites they seized was Chernobyl, briefly leading the international community to worry, amidst fear that shelling might damage the New Safe Confinement structure and a sudden rise in radiation levels. Some also expressed concern that the Russians would plunder the decommissioned plant's hundreds of tonnes of spent nuclear fuel for use in some sinister operation. However, it later became clear that the seizure of Chernobyl was purely strategic; the plant lies on the main highway from Russia's ally Belarus to Kyiv and Putin's forces took the site as part of a wider plan to secure a key attack route into the Ukrainian capital.

The ill effects of Chernobyl continue to reverberate around the world more than 35 years after the accident. Environmentally, they will be felt for hundreds if not thousands of years. The accident adversely affected the way that many people view nuclear power, causing the industry to lose ground to greener sources of energy at a time when fossil fuels were becoming increasingly unpopular with consumers. If Chernobyl had not happened, nuclear power stations would surely be providing much more of the world's electricity than the 10 per cent that they do today.

The accident polluted Europe's air, poisoned the land and left death and destruction in its wake, but the truly terrible thing about the disaster was that it was entirely preventable. More than once during the night of 26 April 1986, the operators in Chernobyl's Unit 4 reactor control room faced circumstances where they should have abandoned the turbine test they were carrying out but did not. This was the human element of the accident. Even so, it is the technical aspect of the reactor's failure that was far more significant. The known and accepted design flaw at the heart of the Soviet Union's RBMK nuclear reactors – all of them, and not just those as Chernobyl – represented the inherent dysfunction that underpinned, and eventually undid, the Soviet Union. In retrospect, it seems inevitable that, of all the world's nuclear power stations, it was the reactor at a Soviet plant that would fail so disastrously, and in doing so help bring about the conditions for the destruction of the system that created it.

Epilogue:
THE FUKUSHIMA DISASTER

When it comes to safety at a nuclear power plant, you can train operators to be better prepared for unexpected events, or to deal with difficult situations more competently. You can also build better, safer nuclear reactors, fitted with protective measures in the event of mechanical failures or technical problems. But one thing it is much more difficult to guard against is the destructive power of nature. This was illustrated to devastating effect in March 2011, at the Fukushima Daiichi nuclear power station in Okuma, Japan, 220km (137 miles) north of Toyko, when the plant was inundated by a 14m/46ft-high tsunami that knocked out the station's power systems and caused a partial reactor meltdown that is recognized as the second worst nuclear accident in history.

In the official International Nuclear Event Scale (INES) table of measurement, which gauges nuclear accidents by number from 1 (Anomaly) to 7 (Major Accident), only Fukushima and Chernobyl have been certified at the highest grade. Chernobyl is still by far the worst accident, having released 10 times more radiation than Fukushima and killed more people, but that's not to downplay the severity of the Japanese incident in any way. If anything, it illustrates just how bad Chernobyl was. If that accident had never happened Fukushima would be an episode far more talked about, the poster child for nuclear disaster. In some respects, it may prove to be a more significant event than Chernobyl, especially in terms of *when* it happened as well as how.

By 2011 most countries in the world had accepted that the earth's supply of fossil fuels was not going to last forever. Oil and natural gas supplies were running out and other energy sources had to be developed. For a long time, nuclear power was very much the heir apparent – until Chernobyl dented its popularity. Even so, most developed nations, and, increasingly, developing ones, pressed on with nuclear power programmes. In the 1980s wind and solar power were seen as the preserve of cranks and eco-warriors. No one had even heard of biomass, and geothermal energy was one of those 'it'll never work' technologies that eccentric boffins laboured over in their garden sheds at night. Hydroelectricity was entering the mainstream, but what about those countries where water was scarce? In short, renewable, carbon-free or carbon-neutral energy sources were a long way off, a dream for the future.

By 2011, and in part inspired by the Chernobyl disaster, that future had arrived. Those alternative power sources were now available, and it was time to choose. The Fukushima accident served as a reminder of what was at stake and focused the minds of energy policymakers around the world into making definitive, difficult decisions about which directions their countries were going to take. Stick with nuclear power, abandon it in favour of renewables, or forge some sort of compromise between the two? And if nuclear power was not finished yet, how could it be made safer?

Japan sits across one of the most active zones of the Ring of Fire, the rough circle around the Pacific where Earth's tectonic plates are in constant, often volatile, movement. As a result, it's an area of intense volcanic and earthquake activity. Japan experiences on average 1,500 earthquakes each year, most of them minor, with scores of tremors every day. This has had a profound effect on the country's life and culture. Japan's traditional architecture of low-level, flexible, wooden buildings, for example, evolved in part to help prevent the daily seismic activity shaking its buildings into piles of rubble. In the modern era, Japan has been at the forefront of earthquake engineering. The architect and engineer Tachū Naitō is credited with inventing the earthquake-proof wall – concrete and steel-reinforced partitions that act as shear walls, designed to absorb earthquake shockwaves. This concept revolutionized structural engineering, making buildings in earthquake zones – even tall buildings – safer than ever before. Japanese buildings have for decades been constructed with earthquake safety in mind, but, in Fukushima's case, this was not enough.

The 9.0-magnitude earthquake struck 72km (45 miles) off Japan's Pacific coast, close to the city of Sendai, at 2.40 p.m. on 11 March 2011. It lasted for six terrifying minutes and was the largest earthquake that had ever hit Japan – and one of the most powerful ever, so much so that it caused our planet to tilt off its axis by 17cm (6.6in), shortening an Earth day by 1.8 microseconds (one microsecond being one millionth of a second). Whole towns and beachfront resorts were destroyed.

So much energy was released that a tsunami wave hundreds of kilometres long sped across the ocean up to 800km/h (500 mph), crashing into the Japanese mainland just 10 minutes after the earthquake. Few people living and working along the coast where the tsunami first hit had the time or the wherewithal to evacuate themselves to a safer place. More than 18,000 people were killed along a swathe of coastline at least 200km (124 miles) long. This was undoubtedly a terrible catastrophe, but it very quickly became apparent that the earthquake and tsunami could very well have triggered a monumentally disastrous event.

The Fukushima Daiichi nuclear power station was commissioned in 1971, around the same time as Chernobyl. Unlike that power station, though, Fukushima used boiling water reactors (BWRs). These worked on the same principle as the Soviet RBMK reactors, with nuclear fission inside the reactor heating water so that it turned into steam, which in turn drove a series of electricity-generating turbines. One advantage of Fukushima's six reactors over Chernobyl's was that they were surrounded by protective pressure vessels. As at the Three Mile Island disaster (*see* Prologue), these pressure vessels stopped the accident that followed the tsunami strike being much worse than was possible by containing some of the radiation once it began to escape from the failing reactor core.

Because the plant was located in an area of intense seismic activity, it was built with features that, in 'normal', i.e. less intense, earthquake situations, would probably have worked reasonably well. But the March 2011 episode was so out of the ordinary that they were simply overwhelmed. This failure to anticipate the extraordinary was the cause of some criticism, as we will see below; there are many experts who claim that, even in the face of one of the most powerful earthquakes ever recorded, there were measures that should have been in place to stop Fukushima's nuclear reactors from melting down.

As it was, once the earthquake was detected, emergency systems automatically shut down the three reactors at the plant then in operation: Units 1, 2 and 3. At the moment the reactors were shut down, emergency backup diesel generators switched themselves on and began pumping coolant water into the reactors' fuel cores to stop them from overheating. So far, everything had run according to plan; the plant's crisis response systems had detected a problem and dealt with it in the way they were designed to do. But, once the tsunami hit, 11 of the 12 emergency generators on site were instantly submerged in water and knocked out of action. This was not an immediate problem because the tsunami flooded the nuclear reactors, too, preventing them from overheating. But once the seawater began to recede, the reactors' fuel cores heated up once more, and this time the backup generators could not fulfil their role; they were still disabled.

Over the next three days Fukushima's three damaged reactors became more and more unstable as uncontrolled nuclear fission heated up their fuel cores to dangerously high temperatures. Meltdown was underway. Plant workers and emergency services teams tried to take action, but the site was in a state of upheaval. Hydrogen gas escaping from the damaged reactors began to explode, turning the plant into something resembling a war zone. And there was more. As the International Atomic Energy Agency (IAEA) report on the accident response pointed out, 'work was conducted in extremely poor conditions, with uncovered manholes and cracks and depressions in the ground. Work at night was conducted in the dark. There were many obstacles blocking access to the road such as debris from the tsunami and rubble that was produced by the explosions that occurred in Units 1, 3 and 4. All work was conducted with respirators and protective clothing and mostly in high radiation fields.'

Unable to securely contain the damaged reactors, the authorities ordered an immediate evacuation of the area and 150,000 people were forced to move beyond an exclusion zone 20km (12 miles) around the plant as radiation leaked into to the atmosphere.

This was a precaution learned from Chernobyl. As with the Ukrainian accident, the zone's boundary was a somewhat arbitrary figure, however. In the first days after the Fukushima meltdown, it was not clear how much radiation had been released. Nuclear physicists analyzing the data in real time believed the Fukushima meltdown was not as bad as that at Chernobyl, so 20km appeared a workable solution. The experts were correct, as it turned out; Fukushima released one-tenth of the amount of radiation emitted by Chernobyl. Japan's population is three times that of Ukraine's and is densely concentrated along its eastern coast. Ordering a clearance of anything greater than a 20km radius around Fukushima would have caused an unmanageable migration of perhaps a million people or more. In addition, the entire coastline for at least 100km (62 miles) in either direction up and down from Fukushima was a disaster area, too. While much of the emergency response to the earthquake and tsunami had centred around the beleaguered nuclear power station, there were cities, towns, villages and, of course, millions of scared, homeless, injured and bewildered Japanese in need of attention.

The government's resources were severely stretched, the state's fire crews, police, army and emergency services working non-stop, exhausted and following protocols that were being devised on the go and in chaotic circumstances. Up to 500,000 people in total were displaced by the earthquake, so when the populace around Fukushima were told to leave the area, it was not immediately clear where they were supposed to go – were they simply moving out of one disaster area and into another?

It was not until 16 December 2011 that the Fukushima Daiichi nuclear power station was officially brought back under control, when a state of 'cold shutdown' was declared. This meant that the plant operators had managed to stop reactivity taking place in all of the damaged Units, and that all further radiation released at the site would be residual rather than ongoing and active. Remarkably, no one died at the plant during the tsunami, although up to 20 personnel were injured by the explosions and fires that ravaged the site. Radiation would later affect dozens of Fukushima's workers and emergency personnel, but only one person is so far is known to have died from its effects. In 2018, Japan's Ministry of Health, Labour and Welfare confirmed that an unnamed worker who had been engaged in the clean-up operation had died from lung cancer caused by radiation

Workers in protective clothing prepare to clean the site after the reactor meltdown at Fukushima.

exposure. This employee was just one of the so-called Fukushima 50, the operatives sent into the plant to contain the accident and begin the clean-up. Despite the name, there were hundreds of personnel engaged in this dangerous enterprise. Their identities have been kept secret and the Fukushima 50 have become mysterious, almost mythic figures in Japan, lauded as archetypes of what a Japanese citizen should be: public spirited, selfless and self-effacing.

In the longer term, a 2013 World Health Organization study on Fukushima concluded that the disaster will not lead to an increase in cancer rates in the region. This is because a large portion of the radiation released during the accident was blown out into the Pacific Ocean rather than inland. This stands in stark contrast to Chernobyl, where the prevailing winds sent the

disaster's radiation cloud billowing north and west across much of Ukraine, Belarus, Russia and large areas of Europe, reaching as far as Ireland, more than 3,000km (1,860 miles) away.

But not all of Fukushima's radiation drifted off to sea. More than a decade after Fukushima, many of the towns and settlements within its exclusion zone remain uninhabited, with radiation levels at unacceptably high levels – although in some cases this can vary quite dramatically within a small area. The town of Tomioka, 10km (6 miles) from Fukushima, is an extreme example of this. Tomioka was evacuated directly after the meltdown, but in 2017 its former inhabitants were allowed to come home. Not all of them did, put off perhaps by the fact that 12 per cent of Tomioka remained off limits to humans because it is still heavily irradiated. Part of this no-go area was used as a temporary dump for radioactive soil, vegetation and other material collected from the town following the accident, and it remained littered with black bin bags filled with toxic debris awaiting collection and transportation to a safe disposal site. It's a similar story in areas such as Namie and Iitate, two towns close to Fukushima that were bombarded with some of the highest levels of radiation during the disaster. As of 2021, their combined population was 1,200, down from 28,000 before the accident. Both towns are dotted with areas of dilapidation and decay, too toxic for human habitation, among zones of urban regeneration where old residents have returned from their nuclear exile or new populations are moving in. These are people who have come home because they were never properly resettled after their evacuation or because they have nowhere else to go.

Fukushima is not exactly Japan's dirty secret, but it is an event on which both the government and the wider public prefer not to dwell. There is a sense in Japanese society that the subject is over, and it is time to move on. By 2021 the country had spent $27 billion cleaning up after the 2011 earthquake in general and the Fukushima disaster in particular. Armies of workers, an almost 80,000-strong force akin to the liquidators of Chernobyl, had spent months decontaminating buildings, cutting down poisoned forests and digging up toxic, dead soil in the exclusion zone. Once this was done, the story of Fukushima was – at least in many people's minds – over.

All that remains now is to deal with the Fukushima Daiichi nuclear power plant itself. This is a much slower process. As at Chernobyl, the nuclear reactors are being carefully disassembled and the plant's buildings cleansed and pulled down. In time, decades perhaps, the site will be completely cleared. Whether the land there will ever be usable again is unclear. It is highly unlikely, but such is the need for space in Japan's crowded and populous islands that who knows how future definitions of what constitutes 'safe' and 'acceptable' levels of radiation may be adjusted or manipulated to help the country cope with its demographic priorities.

At the time of the Fukushima accident, it was usually described as a natural disaster or an act of God. While Japan's government and the plant's owners are keen to stick to this narrative, there are credible arguments to be made that the incident was in fact avoidable, or that at least its worst effects could have been ameliorated if better safety measures and earthquake planning had been put in place.

The first thing critics point to is the power station's location. Nuclear reactors need water, and lots of it. This is why they are always close to rivers and lakes, or situated along coastlines. Indeed, 25 per cent of the world's nuclear power stations are located on the coast, and Fukushima Daiichi was just one, thirstily sucking up hundreds of thousands of litres of seawater each day to provide liquid for the six reactors' coolant systems and supply the water that was pumped through the reactor cores to be boiled into the steam that drove the plant's electricity-generating turbines. When the plant's site was first selected, it was an area of flat ground on a high bluff, or cliff, overlooking the sea; some 3.5km^2 (860 acres) standing 35m (115ft) above sea level. As plans for the power station developed, the plant owners, Tokyo Electric Power Company (TEPCO), decided to lower the cliff face by 25m (82ft) so that the building foundations could be sunk more deeply into the bedrock, in theory making the plant buildings more stable in the event of an earthquake. Moving the plant closer to sea level also meant that running costs could be saved because the pumps would not have to work as hard or as long to transport water from the sea to the reactors. Building the nuclear power station just 10m (32ft) above sea level made it far more susceptible to tidal waves and tsunamis, however, and this design flaw was compounded by the decision to place the backup diesel generators in a basement area beneath the reactors. When the tsunami hit on 11 March 2011, the plant never stood a chance. A protective sea wall had been put up in front of the power station, but it was not high enough and was easily overwhelmed. In 2012 nuclear energy analysts at the influential Carnegie Endowment for International Peace issued a report on the accident and were unequivocal about Fukushima's lack of preparedness for any danger from the sea: 'The Fukushima Daiichi Nuclear Power Station was not designed to withstand a tsunami even half the size of the one that ultimately struck the Japanese coast in March 2011.'

It has since been recommended that coastal nuclear power stations, especially those in locations prone to flooding and intense seismic activity, should be built on high ground, away from all but the most freakish of tidal waves or tsunamis. At the very least, the backup generators for managing nuclear reactor cooling systems should be located away from the main site and in raised areas, or housed in watertight bunkers.

Expert commentators insist there are other ways where Fukushima's owners TEPCO and Japan's regulatory body, the Nuclear and Industrial Safety Agency (NISA), could have acted more responsibly. In their accident report, the Carnegie authors argued that TEPCO and NISA fell below international safety standards by allowing the plant to be built without paying enough attention to tsunami flood risks and by not doing enough computer modelling to assess how seismic events and flooding could impact the power station site. The Carnegie writers also pointed out that NISA did not have enough regulatory power to enforce greater safety conditions, even if they had recommended any, and that there was in Japan too great an emphasis on making buildings earthquake-proof at the expense of making them tsunami-proof as well. Tsunamis are admittedly rare, so it's understandable that paying attention to earthquake damage takes a higher priority than preparing for flooding, but it appears that Fukushima's builders believed the possibility of flooding was too remote a possibility to consider seriously.

That said, it was also revealed after the accident that Fukushima's earthquake defences were not up to industry standard anyway. TEPCO denied this had any bearing on the course of the disaster and that all of the damage at the plant was flood-related, but it did not reflect well on the power station's owners or on NISA for failing to enforce the necessary safety measures required to manage a nuclear facility properly.

Just weeks before the accident NISA approved a request by TEPCO to extend Fukushima Daiichi's operating life by 10 years (by Japanese law, its nuclear power stations much get special dispensation to remain active for more than 40 years, and 2011 was the plant's fortieth birthday). It is not clear if NISA carried out a full review of Fukushima's safety features or made any recommendations for improving them beforehand, but TEPCO did not have any security upgrades in progress when the accident happened. By the terms of its licence extension, TEPCO was obliged to monitor the ongoing condition of some of its reactors' components and machinery, but that appeared to be the extent of the conditions placed upon the plant owners in order to carry on operating.

After the accident, the head of Japan's Nuclear Safety Commission put a request before the country's parliament for a review of seismic safety guidelines. Fukushima was a rare event, but it did happen – and given Japan's geography and geology there is no guarantee it will be a one-off. In July 2013 new regulations were introduced in Japan to force nuclear power station operators to strengthen their safety measures against earthquakes and tsunamis, so that they are better able to withstand what are known as 'beyond-design events' – namely, accidents and problems of a greater magnitude than anticipated when the plant was originally built.

The disaster at Fukushima had profound effects on the nuclear power industry in Japan. Before the accident the country was one of the world's leading advocates of nuclear energy, and 30 per cent of Japan's electricity was generated in nuclear power stations. Plans were in progress to increase that to 40 per cent. Following the accident, all of the country's 54 reactors were closed for inspection; as of 2021 just nine of those reactors were operating again, the rest either still being assessed or scheduled for decommission. The public's approval rating for nuclear energy in Japan plummeted to just 20 per cent after the accident and has been falling ever since. In March 2020 the Japan Atomic Energy Relations Organization (JAERO) published the results of a national survey showing that 49.4 per cent of people wanted to phase out nuclear power, while just 11 per cent viewed it favourably as an energy source. Japan may still need its nuclear power stations for a while yet – and it may even build some new ones – but these do not represent the future of the country's energy policy. In the run-up to the COP26 United Nations Climate Change Conference held in Glasgow, Scotland, in October/November 2021, Japan announced that it was aiming to generate 20–30 per cent of its electricity from nuclear power by 2030. This is unlikely, given the unpopularity of nuclear power and the lack of nuclear power stations currently in operation there. It is possible the country will try instead to raise its target for using renewables to generate electricity, from its current plan of 36–38 per cent. The Fukushima accident may not have directly killed any humans but it pretty much killed the Japanese nuclear power industry.

Today, nuclear energy remains a contentious and contradictory issue. In general terms it is safe to produce, but when accidents do happen they may be catastrophic with long-lasting and far-reaching implications, as at Chernobyl and Fukushima. While it's not a renewable source of energy, nuclear power is, in some respects, Green. It produces no harmful emissions, for example, though the impact on the environment of building nuclear power stations, mining the uranium that is used for fuel in most of them, and disposing of that fuel safely once it had been used are divisive issues.

For many years nuclear energy was seen as the solution to the vexed question of which fuel source would eventually replace the world's dwindling and polluting supplies of fossil fuels such as oil and gas. But uranium supplies are finite, too, although they can be reprocessed and reused, with diminishing returns each time. It's estimated there are enough uranium deposits to keep the world's nuclear power station supplied for another 80 years. It is at best, then, a stopgap energy source. The question today is for how long it will remain in use for; presumably until longer-lasting renewable sources such as wind power, biomass and solar energy become the norm.

While Japan weans itself off nuclear energy, it can look to Germany as an example of a developed nation that is well on the road to going nuclear-free. As the home of one of the world's most successful Green parties, and one which came to prominence as a direct result of the Chernobyl disaster, Germany is firmly in the anti-nuclear energy camp. The country committed itself to moving away from nuclear power as far back as 2002. In 2011 Germany's chancellor Angela Merkel stepped up the country's decommissioning plans, setting a deadline of 2022 for the shutdown of the last of its nuclear power stations. By 2021 Germany had just six plants left open, and in December of that year closed three of them for good. This has had other implications, though. Until it significantly improves its provision of renewable resources, Germany has been forced to begin burning more coal again to replace the energy shortfall left by the closure of its nuclear power stations.

Germany's move away from nuclear energy has had wider, political implications, too. As Russian troops massed on Ukraine's border in late 2021 and early 2022 during the international crisis that developed there, Germany's hesitation in standing four-square behind its US and European allies in condemning Moscow's act of aggression was believed in part to have been motivated by Germany's need for Russian natural gas. As the crisis in Ukraine developed, it coincided with the completion of the Nord Stream 2 project, a pipeline constructed and managed by Russia's majority state-owned Gazprom energy supplier that was designed to provide millions of German homes and businesses with Russian natural gas. At the time of writing, Germany's government had not given Gazprom the go-ahead to begin supplying gas, caught as the country was between the desire to satisfy its energy needs and its obligations to stand with other NATO nations against Russian provocation in Ukraine.

Germany's political and power supply dilemmas provide an, admittedly extreme, example of why most other nations are not ready to abandon nuclear energy just yet – and indeed while some are actively increasing their interest in it. The United States has been the biggest producer of nuclear-powered electricity for many years, operating 93 reactors across 30 states. Thirty per cent of global nuclear energy is produced in American reactors, and they account for 20 per cent of electricity generated for the domestic US market. However, most of these reactors are coming to the end of their operating lives. The majority were built in the 1960s and early 1970s, and the Three Mile Island accident of 1979 prevented new construction work on any reactors until 2013, when engineers embarked on the expansion of the existing Alvin W. Vogtle Electric Generating Plant in Georgia, where two new reactors are being added to the two already in operation.

What this indicates is that the United States is no longer at the forefront of the modern nuclear industry. That honour is being contested between France and China, although neither country has had a spectacularly great track record in nuclear power development in the post-Fukushima era. At its height in the early 2000s, France had 56 operational nuclear reactors, generating up to 70 per cent of the country's energy, the highest proportion in the world. Around a quarter of that power was generated using recycled nuclear fuel and France is planning to build more reactors using reprocessed fuel in the coming years. However, as of early 2022, around one fifth of France's reactors had been shut down, suffering mainly from corrosion, leaving the country's energy output at its lowest levels since the 1990s – and forcing France to turn to its coal-fired power stations once more.

France's efforts to invest in nuclear power overseas have been less than stellar, too. France's largely state-owned energy company EDF is behind the Hinkley Point C nuclear power station in Somerset, England, whose opening date has, at the last estimate, been moved from 2025 to 2026 and whose cost has spiralled from an original estimate of £4–5 billion to at least £23 billion. Hinkley C is supposed to represent the next generation of nuclear reactors, but the late delivery date, its ever-growing price tag and persistent rumours of ongoing technical problems with the reactor design (which is also being used on at least one new EDF project in China) have cast a shadow over what is one of the largest infrastructure projects in the UK. Hinkley C is part of the UK's programme to increase its nuclear-generated electricity from 21 per cent to 25 per cent by the late 2020s, a modest increase reflecting that fact that Britain is a relatively small-time player in the nuclear power market, operating just 15 reactors in total.

China has adopted a similar strategy to France of ramping up its commitment to nuclear energy at home and abroad. Its 51 reactors generate just 5 per cent of the country's electricity, but there are at least another 18 reactors under construction, with 39 more planned, and China is actively partnering with overseas nations to help build their nuclear power capacity, too. This is part of the state's policy of economic imperialism, investing heavily in developing countries such as Bangladesh, Pakistan and Egypt, as well as better-off nations such as the United Arab Emirates and, controversially, the United Kingdom, where the Chinese-owned China General Nuclear (CGN) and France's EDF have taken a 20 per cent and 80 per cent share respectively in building the proposed $20 billion Sizewell C plant on the

Suffolk coast. In late 2021 the British government announced it was trying to force CGN to relinquish its interest in the project, but at the time of writing it had not been able to achieve this. Agreements were signed when the government (like many in the West) was less wary of China, a country now viewed as a political, economic and technological rival.

Yet while China is actively attempting to insert itself into other nations' nuclear energy infrastructures, it is also devising interesting strategies to make its own nuclear energy programmes independent and closed to outside influence. Using components and technologies that rival nations have not yet worked out how to replicate, its domestically produced Hualong One and Hualong Two pressurized water reactors are said to be safer and more efficient than existing, Western reactor designs – although we only have China's word for that. Nuclear power experts advise viewing the country's claims with a large amount of scepticism until proven otherwise. More intriguingly, China has looked at accidents such as Chernobyl and Fukushima and is exploring alternative nuclear fuel sources. Where most nations with nuclear reactors use uranium and water in their operation, China is spending billions of dollars prototyping reactors that employ the radioactive element thorium as their fuel and molten salt as their coolant. Thorium is in plentiful supply in China and this, along with its home-made Hualong reactors, would make the country self-sufficient in its nuclear power needs if the technology can be made to work. Having learned no doubt from Ukraine's dependence on Russian uranium, and the political and military troubles this has caused, China is demonstrating, not for the first time, how much of a keen student of history she is.

Since the Three Mile Island accident of 1979, nuclear power's reputation has endured some torrid times. As the dominance of fossil fuels as an energy source began to wane from the 1980s onwards, many in the nuclear power industry thought their time had come at last – only for Chernobyl and then Fukushima to do their cause huge, possibly irreparable, harm. With environmentalism becoming an increasingly pressing issue since the new millennium, interest in using green, renewable sources of energy has moved firmly into the mainstream, and advocates of nuclear energy have been forced onto the defensive once more.

While its cheerleaders claim that nuclear power is safe and clean, events have a terrible habit of periodically proving that this is not, strictly speaking, true. Unless we properly learn from tragedies such as Chernobyl, atomic energy disasters will keep coming. And as nuclear plants get larger, more powerful and increasingly complex, so the prospect of ever-more massive disasters becomes more likely. To date, Chernobyl is the worst nuclear power accident the world has ever seen. Hopefully, it always will be.

TIMELINE

1970

20 February: Work begins on building the Chernobyl nuclear power plant

1977

26 September: The first of Chernobyl's four nuclear reactors begins to generate electricity

1986

26 April: at 1.23.58 am Chernobyl's Unit 4 reactor explodes. The emergency services arrive within 10 minutes. By early morning members of an investigatory and clean-up group, the Shcherbina Commission, arrive from Moscow

27 April: 50,000 people are evacuated from the nearby town of Pripyat

28 April: Sweden's Forsmark Nuclear Power Plant detects higher than normal atmospheric radiation levels, indicating a major incident has taken place; the Soviet Union refuses to confirm or deny this

29 April: Radio Free Europe breaks the story of an accident at Chernobyl; on the accident site, helicopters begin attempting to put out the Unit 4 reactor fire; the Soviet Union declines America's help in dealing with its as-yet unconfirmed accident

1 May: Soviet leader Mikhail Gorbachev orders May Day celebrations to go ahead in Kyiv, close to the accident site, against the wishes of local Ukrainian leaders

2 May: 30km (19 mile) exclusion zone around Chernobyl established

5 May: Unit 4 reactor fire extinguished after 10 days; possible *China Syndrome* situation identified in the damaged reactor, which is only narrowly averted; G7 nations issue a joint statement urging the Soviet Union to admit a serious accident has taken place; Soviet state news agency TASS confirms the accident's extent for the first time

9 May: Hans Blix, the International Atomic Energy Agency (IAEA) director, visits Chernobyl

14 May: Mikhail Gorbachev makes a public broadcast to acknowledge the accident to the Soviet people

3 July: The Shcherbina Commission report into the accident is discussed at a secret meeting before Mikhail Gorbachev in Moscow

19 July: The Soviet TV news show *Vremya* officially blames the accident on human error

25 August: the scientist and Shcherbina Commission member Valery Legasov presents a wide-ranging account of the accident to the IAEA in Vienna, to public acclaim

1 November: the first 'Sarcophagus' is built around the ruined Unit 4 reactor at Chernobyl

1987

8-29 July: the trial takes place in Chernobyl of the six defendants held responsible for the accident; all six are found guilty and imprisoned

1988

27 April: Suicide of Valery Legasov

1989

24 February: Mikhail Gorbachev visits Chernobyl for the first
and only time
9 November: Fall of the Berlin Wall

1991

19 August: A failed coup is launched against Mikhail Gorbachev
24 August: Gorbachev resigns as Communist Party leader;
Ukraine declares independence
25 December: Gorbachev resigns as President and formally
dissolves the Soviet Union

2000

15 December: Chernobyl closes for good

2019

3 July: Replacement sarcophagus, known as the New Safe
Confinement structure, is completed

INDEX

Abagian, Armen 95
Akimov, Aleksand
    accident at Chernobyl 56, 57, 60, 61,
    63, 71, 72
    containment and clean–up operation
    81
    death of 169
    investigation into accident 119
    trial over accident 140, 141, 144, 145
Aleksandrov, Anatolii
    investigation into accident 124, 125,
    126, 127, 129
    nuclear power in Soviet Union 28,
    29, 33
    retirement 172
Aliyev, Heydar 162
Andropov, Yuri 42, 180
Ananenko, Alexey 109
Antoshkin, Nikolai 102, 103, 104
Bailey, William J 11
Baker, Kenneth 159
Baklanov, Oleg 181
Baranov, Boris 109
Becquerel, Henri 10
Belokon, Valentin 83, 84
Berdov, Hennadii 91
Bespalov, Valery 109
Black Sea 26–7
Blix, Hans 164–6, *167*
Bodie 217–18
Brazhnik, Vyacheslav 68
Brezhnev, Leonid 178, 179
Brize, Raimond 140, 146
Bryukhanov, Valentina 35, 37, 150
Bryukhanov, Viktor *36*
    accident at Chernobyl 46–7, 50, 56,
    71, 72, 75–6, 77–80
    building of Chernobyl 34–5, 37–8,
    41, 42, 43, 44

    building of Pripyat 40
    containment and clean–up operation
    85–7, 89, 91
    death of 147
    investigation into accident 119, 131
    rehabilitation of 212
    trial over accident 139, 140–3, 144,
    146
Brzezinsk, Zbigniew 26–7
Budapest Memorandum 204, 205
Byers, Eben 11
Byrnes, John 20
Carter, Jimmy 27
Catherine the Great 165
Chernenko, Konstantin 180
Chernobyl nuclear reactor
    accident at 46–7, 49–79
    building of 34–8, 41–2
    containment and clean–up operation
    81–115
    costs of accident 149–56, 168–74, 223
    decommissioning of 205–6
    decontamination of 214, 216
    early problems at 42–6
    entombing of 104, 165, 206–10,
    213–14
    international reaction to accident
    100–2, 133–8, 156–9, 160–8, 187,
    188–91
    investigation into accident 117–37
    political reaction to accident 161,
    162, 163, 166, 168, 184–7, 191
    trial over accident 138–47
    use after accident 201–2, 211–12
Chicago Pile-1 13, 14
China Syndrome, The 22
Cockcroft, Sir John 19
Cuban Missile Crisis 178
Curie, Marie 10

Curie, Pierre 10
Daily Express 101
Daily Mail 101–2
Daily Telegraph 175
Dally, Clarence 9
Dollezhal, Nikolai
   nuclear power in Soviet Union 28,
     29–30, 32–3, 118–19, 177
Douglas, Michael 22
Dyatlov, Anatoly
   accident at Chernobyl 50–1, 52, 56,
     57, 58, 60, 62, 63, 67–8, 69–71, 72,
     74–5, 77, 78, 95
   containment and clean–up operation
     86–7, 91
   investigation into accident 119, 131
   trial over accident 139, 141, 144–5,
     146–7
Edison, Thomas 9, 10
Experimental Breeder Reactor I (EBR-I)
   15–16, *17*
Fermi, Enrico 13
Financial Times 101
Fomin, Nikolai
   accident at Chernobyl 71, 72, 75
   containment and clean–up operation
     88
   investigation into accident 119
   trial over accident 139, 140–1, 143–4,
     146
Fonda, Jane 22
Forsmark Nuclear Power Plant 100
Frasyniuk, Wladyslaw 190
Freedom and Peace organization 190
Fukushima nuclear accident 227–41
Gazin, Sergei 70
Gorbachenko, Nikolai 68–9
Gorbachev, Mikhail *183*
   containment and clean–up operation
     88, 100, 105
   costs of accident 150, 160
   dissolution of Soviet Union 197,
     198–9
   entombing of Chernobyl 104, 206–7
   expansion of nuclear power in Soviet
     Union 43
   as General Secretary of Communist
     Party 44, 100, 161, 181–2, 192, 193,

     194
   investigation into accident 125, 126,
     127–9, 130
   political reaction to accident 161,
     162, 163, 166, 168, 184–5, 191
   trial over accident 143
Grand Duchy of Moscow 26
Gromyko, Andrei 161, 181
Hinkley C nuclear power station 244
Hiroshima 12, 13
Hladush, Ivan 95
Institute of Atomic Energy 29
International Atomic Energy Agency
   (IAEA) 122, 133–8, 164, 165, 232
Japan Atomic Energy Relations
   Organization
   (JAERO) 240
Kalugin, Alexander 120, 122
KGB 45–6, 50, 170
Khodemchuk, Valery 65–6, 168–9
Khrushchev, Nikita 29, 178
Kievan Rus' 25, 34
Kommunist 33, 119
Kovalenko, Alexander 140, 145, 146
Kovalevskaia, Liubov 44, 45
Kryuchkov, Vladimir 181, 198
Kuchma, Leonid 206, 212
Kudryavtsev, Aleksandr 62, 63, 66, 72,
   145
Kurchatov, Igor 28, 177
Kurchatov Institute of Atomic Energy 93,
   120, 123–4, 141, 172, 173, 177
Kyshtym nuclear accident 16, 18
Kyzyma, Vasyl
   building of Chernobyl 37–8, 41, 43,
     44–5
   building of Pripyat 40
   containment and clean–up operation
     88
   trial over accident 146
Laushkin, Yuri 140, 145, 146
Legasov, Valery *121*
   containment and clean–up operation
     93, 107, 108–9
   costs of accident on 171–4
   evacuation of Pripyat 94–6
   investigation into accident 118, 120,
     122–3, 129, 133–8

Sarcophagus entombing 104
Legg, Richard C 20
Lelechenko, Aleksandr 74
Lenin, Vladimir 26, 165
Leningrad Nuclear Power Plant 32, 119
Liashko, Oleksandr 91, 161
Ligachev, Yegor 105, 106
Liutov, Mikhail 77
Maiorets, Anatolii 43
    containment and clean-up operation
    89, 91–2, 105
    investigation into accident 124, 126,
    128, 129, 131, 134
Makar, Ivan 193
Malomuzh, Volodymyr 75, 87
Manhattan Project 13
Marin, Vladimir
    containment and clean–up operation
    89
MAUD Committee 13
Mayak nuclear accident 16, 18
McKinley , Richard Leroy 20
Merkel, Angela 242
Meshkov, Aleksandr 102–3, 119, 128,
    129, 131
Nagasaki 12, 13
Naitō, Tachū 229
Naka, Midori 12
National Radiological Protection Board
    19
Neporozhny, Petro 35
New York Times 10
Nuclear and Industrial Safety Agency
(NISA) 238–9
Operation Cyclone 187
Organization of Arab Petroleum
Exporting Countries (OPEC) 23
Palamarchuk, Pyotr 68–9
Parashin, Sergei 75, 78, 79
Perevozchenko, Valery 65, 66, 68, 72
Petrosyants, Andranik 122, 133
Polushkin, Konstantin 92
Pravyk, Nadya 96
Pravyk, Volodymyr 82, 83, 85
Pripyat
    in arrested decay 217–22
    building of 35, 37
    evacuation of 87, 91, 94–100, 102,

150
    growth of 38–41
Proskuryakov, Viktor 62, 63, 66, 72, 145
Prushinsky, Boris 92
Putin, Vladimir 27, 225
Radiendocrinator 11
Radithor 11
Radio Free Europe 101
Radio Liberty 101
Radium Girls 11–12
Reagan, Ronald 182
Richardson, Bill 212
Rogozhkin, Boris 139–40, 141, 145, 146
Röntgen, Wilhelm 9, 10
Rukh 194, 195, 197, 198
Ryzhkov, Nikolai
    ally of Gorbachev 181
    containment and clean–up operation
    105, 106
    entombing of Chernobyl 210
    evacuation of Pripyat 95
    investigation into accident 134–5, 138
    political reaction to accident 162
Sevastopol 224
Shadrin, Yurii 140
Shasharin, Gennady
    containment and clean-up operation
    89, 102–3
    investigation into accident 125–6,
    128, 131
Shashenok, Lyudmila 69
Shashenok, Vladimir 68, 69, 169
Shavrey, Leonid 82–3
Shcherbak, Yuriy 195
Shcherban, Oleksandr 34
Shcherbina, Boris
    containment and clean–up operation
    87, 88, 89, 92, 102, 103, 104, 107
    evacuation of Pripyat 95
    investigation into accident 117–18,
    119, 126, 127, 129
    trial over accident 142
Shcherbytsky, Volodymyr 34, 95, 161,
    186, 194
Shevardnadze, Eduard 162, 181
Shishkin, Vladimir 91
Silayev, Ivan 107, 108–9
Sitnikov, Anatoly 75, 76

Sizewell C nuclear power station 244–5
Sklyarov, Vitali 67
Slavsky, Efim
    entombing of Chernobyl 207, 210
    investigation into accident 119–20,
    123, 124, 126, 127–8, 129, 130, 131,
    134
    nuclear power in Soviet Union 28–9,
    32, 33
Slavutych 99, 151, 153, 211
Solidarity (trade union) 190, 195
Soviet Life 67
Stalin, Joseph 165, 175–6
Stationary Low-Power Reactor Number
One (SL-1) nuclear accident 20–1
Sun, The 102
Tarakanov, Nikolai 111, 113
TASS news agency 164
Telyatnikov, Leonid 141
Thatcher, Margaret 182
Three Mile Island nuclear accident 21–4,
    30
Tokyo Electric Power Company
(TEPCO) 237, 238–9
Toptunov, Leonid
    accident at Chernobyl 57–8, 60, 61,
    72
    death of 169
    investigation into accident 119
    trial over accident 140, 141, 145
Trehub, Yurii 51–2, 56–7, 59, 60, 70–1
Uskov, Arkady 76–7
Vorobev, Serafim 78–9
Vremya 101, 132
Waldegrave, William 159
Wall Street Journal 11
Windscale nuclear accident 18–20
Wittmann, Blanche 10
Yanayev, Gennady 181, 198
Yankovsky, Sergei 118, 119, 131, 143
Yaroshinskaya, Alla 195
Yazov, Dimitry 181, 198
Yeltsin, Boris 27
    ally of Gorbachev 181

and coup d'état 198
    investigation into accident 122
Yuvchenko, Sasha 65–7
Zakharov, Anatoli 82
Zborovsky, Piotr 'Moose' 109
Zelenyi Svit (Green World) rally 192–3

PICTURE CREDITS